Independent Medical Coding

Donna Avila-Weil, CMT
and
Rhonda Regan, CCS

Rayve Productions

Rayve Productions Inc.
Box 726 Windsor CA 95492

Cover concept: Alex Weil

Text copyright © 1999 Donna Avila-Weil and Rhonda Regan

Printed in the United States of America

Library of Congress Cataloging-in-Publication Data

Avila-Weil, Donna.
    Independent medical coding--the comprehensive guidebook for career success as a home-based
    medical coder / Donna Avila-Weil and Rhonda Regan.
        p.   cm.
    Includes bibliographical references and index.
    ISBN 1-877810-17-7
    1. Nosology--Code numbers. 2. Home labor. I. Regan, Rhonda, 1957-   . II. Title.
    RB115.A95   1999
    616'.00148--dc21

                                       98-48122
                                         CIP

The authors and publisher thank The American Health Information Management Association (AHIMA) for granting permission to use copyrighted materials in this book.

Dedication from Donna Avila-Weil

To my parents, Patsy Sutton and Bill Azevedo,
with love everlasting

Dedication from Rhonda Regan

To my father, George Ginochio,
with admiration and enormous love

Donna Avila-Weil

Donna Avila-Weil, received her ART credential in 1977, and has worked extensively in the medical record setting for the past 25 years in the areas of coding, medical transcription and in medical staff services. Donna is also a CMT (Certified Medical Transcriptionist) and continues to work and consult as an independent medical transcriptionist.

Donna is a popular keynote speaker, workshop presenter and mentor for novice transcriptionists. In 1991 Donna was honored as Member-of-the-Year by the California Association for Medical Transcription (CAMT). During the past five years, in addition to her other professional pursuits, Donna's career in health care has evolved into the medical staff setting, and she is currently studying for her CMSC (Certified Medical Staff Coordinator) credential.

Donna and her family enjoy a quiet country life in Northern California, where Donna is active in community activities and pursues creative writing in her free time.

Rhonda Regan

Rhonda Regan, has eighteen years experience in the health care field, sixteen of which have been in coding. Rhonda completed her ART course and received her CCS (Certified Coding Specialist) credential from American Health Information Management in 1994.

Rhonda has enjoyed a variety of coding settings throughout her career. She has worked as an assistant director/coding supervisor in a 400 bed acute care facility, DRG coordinator, medical records director in a skilled nursing facility and as an acute care hospital inpatient/outpatient coder.

Rhonda owns her own independent coding and coding/consulting business, presents coding workshops, and was a consultant for a physician-owned-and-developed encoder system.

Rhonda and her two dogs live in Northern California where she enjoys horses and the outdoor country life.

Acknowledgments from
Donna Avila-Weil

Thank you, Rhonda, for agreeing to join me in co-authoring this project, and to Susan Brown, ART, Jeanette Mason, ART, CCS, Mary Smith, and the many contract coders and other specialists for their valuable input and recommendations on this book.

I have bounced a lot of thoughts off of my longtime friend and co-author, Mary Glaccum, CMT, who so kindly allowed us to use some of her writings and resources.

To my six shining stars, Jamie, Tish, Benjie, Keri, Alexis and Jon, I am so grateful that we can share our laughter, love and tears . . . thanks for keeping me "rocking and rolling" all of these years . . . I love you all so very much . . . how much? . . . "Aeons."

Acknowledgments from
Rhonda Regan

A s a novice in the world of publishing, I have been extremely fortunate during the writing of this book, for it could not have been completed without the love and support of a few very special friends.

To Susan Vacca, BFA, AGC . . . thank you for keeping me on track, keeping me laughing, and sharing your profound wisdom.

To Kerry Hein . . . thank you for your wonderful sense of humor and great hugs. Your belief in me has enriched my life immensely.

And finally, to Donna Avila-Weil, my co-author . . . thank you for encouraging me to undertake this opportunity. My deepest appreciation for inspiring me to put my experiences into writing.

CONTENTS

INTRODUCTION

The health care environment has evolved dramatically in the last decade, from the perspective of caring for individual patients to a focus on caring for "populations". Identifying these populations and their health care needs requires review and evaluation of data. This data is used to determine the types of illnesses within the populations, and also to make decisions regarding utilization of resources and costs involved in providing health care to patient populations. One of the major sources for this data entry is the health care coding professional.

The "coder" has evolved from a health information clerical position to a highly technical and specialized field of professionals. To a large extent, health care reimbursement (i.e., payment for health care services) depends on the skills and expertise of health care coding specialists.

Along with the evolution of the coding position, the job description of the coder and the location where coding is performed have also evolved. Coding is no longer a function that is done only in hospitals, or that must be done only in-house or by in-house coders. With the explosion of managed care, coding requirements have expanded to ambulatory care, walk-in clinic, and physician office settings. There are traveling contract coders, coding consultants, home-based coders, optimizers, and numerous other areas where coding expertise is required. Software vendors are developing enhancements to aid the coding of data and that will integrate into the information systems of health care networks. With the need for more and more data, there is a greater demand for coders.

Many coders work for health care facilities and many work independently to provide a variety of coding services to meet the increasing demand for the growing number of coding specialties. Because of the need for accurate coding of data in all of these settings, more and more coding specialists are venturing out on their own to pursue independent careers.

This book has been written to provide useful information regarding business start-ups, resources and alternative coding opportunities for coding specialists to utilize while pursuing successful independent careers. On the following pages we share our knowledge about the coding profession, requirements, benefits, pitfalls and methods of becoming an independent coding specialist. We hope you find it beneficial, and we wish you great success.

WHAT IS CODING?

Coding: The assignment of code(s) to all health data elements of inpatient or outpatient care. All coding systems are encompassed in this definition.

Coding is the process of identification of diagnosis and procedures utilizing a specific classification system, by coding information from the medical records of patients to generate a clinical patient care data base. Accurate and timely coding also assures optimum appropriate reimbursement for the health care facility.

Prior to 1983 there were over 120 different coding systems in use in the United States. In order to bill insurance claims properly the medical practice had to keep track of numerous codes and coding systems, as well as many different claim forms. The complexity of the coding issue was one of the reasons that many practices started giving their patients superbills so that the patient could bill their own insurance. The office staff neither had the time nor the knowledge to bill accurately for the services provided because they weren't sure how to identify the procedure accurately or match it with the appropriate charge. This created tremendous billing errors and often, financial losses for physician practices.

THE HISTORY OF CODING

In 1900, in Geneva, Switzerland, the International List of Causes of Death was first created and adopted for international use. This list was revised periodically, approximately at ten-year intervals.

In 1948, the International List of Causes of Death was revised for the sixth time and published by the World Health Organization as the *Manual of the International Statistical Classification of Diseases, Injuries and Causes of Death*. For the first time many nonfatal disease categories were included.

In 1950, the Public Health Service and the Veterans' Administration started independent tests of the classification for hospital indexing purposes. A year later, the Columbia-Presbyterian Medical Center in New York City adopted the International Classification for this purpose with certain modifications. A few years later, the commission on Professional and Hospital Activities adopted the International Classification, also with similar modifications, for hospitals participating in the Professional Activity Study.

During 1957 the World Health Organization in Geneva, Switzerland developed the *Manual of International Statistical Classification of Diseases, Injuries, and Causes of Death, Volumes 1 and 2*. These manuals documented a system of codes for indexing. The International Classification of Diseases (ICD) was developed for the statistical compilation of diseases and causes of death primarily for the use of public health agencies.

Therefore, in the ICD volumes, diseases are grouped according to the problems they present. For example, the major infective and parasitic diseases are listed in one section and all malignant neoplasms are brought together in another section. A specific disease entity is given a separate title or code number in the classification only when its separation is warranted because of the frequency of its occurrence or its importance as a morbid condition justifies a separate category. Conditions of less importance from this point of view are grouped together, frequently as residual groups of a particular anatomical site or physiological system.

Coding was developed to classify diseases and operations for diagnostic indexing purposes. For hospital indexing purposes, the classification of disease must anticipate every request for patient records in all hospitals and make specific provisions for every diagnostic category.

Originally, coding with three digits covered the major categories or titles with fourth-digit subdivisions used when it was necessary to classify in greater detail. The grouping of related conditions in the ICD coding volumes is recommended for use in hospitals because requests for study materials in hospitals so often follow the same patterns.

Interest in the use of the International Classification for hospital indexing was expressed by the World Health Organization and by many hospitals in the United States. A study was therefore undertaken in 1956 (Efficiency in Hospital Indexing of the Coding System of the International Statistical Classification and Standard Nomenclature of Diseases and Operations) by the American Hospital Association, American Association of Medical Record Librarians, supported by a research grant from the Public Health Service. The study showed that the International Classification of Diseases was highly suitable for hospital indexing.

The first adaptation of the ICD was published in December 1959 as Public Health Service Publication No. 719. This revision was prepared by the Commission on Professional and Hospital Activities under contract with the National Center for Health Statistics of the United States Public Health Service.

As time has passed, more revisions have been required, adding more subdivisions, additional fifth digits, etc. The classification of diseases continues to evolve and will require ongoing revisions.

THE PROSPECTIVE PAYMENT SYSTEM (PPS)

During the early 1980s, the federal government took action to curb spiraling health care costs. Concerned by wide variations in what different hospitals charged to treat the same condition (even though there was no apparent difference in quality of care) and faced with dire forecasts that Medicare was headed toward bankruptcy, Congress determined that the cost of hospital care was rising faster than federal taxes were replenishing the Medicare fund. In 1983, in an effort to solve the problem, Congress mandated a new system that changed the method of payment for hospital care of elderly and disabled Americans. The new plan was called the Prospective Payment System (PPS). The PPS established fixed "prices" for treating specific illnesses and was intended to force hospitals to be more efficient.

DIAGNOSTIC RELATED GROUPS (DRGs)

The PPS paid standard prices for treatment of specific Diagnostic Related Groups (DRGs) in Medicare patients.

The initial inception of the DRG concept was in the late sixties, at Yale University, where they were designed as a utilization management tool, not a payment plan. In 1983, the federal government implemented

Diagnostic Related Groups (DRGs), initially to create an effective framework for monitoring the quality and use of services in a hospital setting. Now coders play a key role in a hospital's financial health, working within the complex environment of the Prospective Payment System. In order to obtain an appropriate DRG assignment, coders must carefully review each medical record with DRG optimizing principles.

THE IMPORTANCE OF ACCURATE MEDICAL CODING IN HEALTH CARE TODAY

Uniform coding of medical and procedural terminology is necessary to allow efficient and meaningful study of diseases, injuries, and other reasons for health care encounters. Medical and procedural terminology is coded to allow study of diseases and procedures.

Coded data was originally intended to be used for research and study but its value has expanded now beyond just the classification of diseases to be the primary key to reimbursement, and statistical analysis by hospitals, insurance companies, health care facilities and other relevant businesses.

THE RESULTS OF CODING

The resulting codes serve two major uses: 1) **statistical**, in which patient information is aggregated by code number, and 2) **clinical**, in which the codes of patients are used individually.

Statistical uses of codes include the study of etiology (cause, origin) and incidences of disease, health care planning and quality control of health care.

The clinical use of codes include completing reimbursement claims and indexing individual patient records, both significant applications in the United States.

THE PURPOSE OF CODING

Quality coding is utilized for an accurate and reliable data base for budgeting, clinical research, credentialing/peer review, education, financial analysis, marketing, patient care, quality assurance/risk management, statistics, strategic planning, utilization management and other internal/external facility purposes.

Coding plays an important role in the health care facility maintaining compliance with licensing, accrediting and regulatory requirements. Coding also supports billing functions of the facility so as to optimize reimbursement through code assignments that are accurate, complete, properly sequenced and timely.

ARE YOU READY TO GO SOLO?

"To be independent is to have wings!"

That wonderful thought of working for oneself may be the driving force for your venturing into independence. What are the motivating factors? More flexibility on the job, no time-card, no clock-watchers looking over your shoulder, no hard-nosed supervisor or resentful coworkers, and mainly because independence gives you the opportunity to expand into new areas, and to be creative.

Do you have what it takes? Most jobs do not allow you the freedom of expression or creativity you would enjoy, because supervisors and managers are often bound by traditional "rules" and "regulations" and, sometimes, they feel threatened by an employee who "outshines" them. When your spirit becomes stifled by the frustration, boredom and hopelessness of your current job, it's time for an entrepreneurial change. You must break away to survive. Hence, independence!

BEING PREPARED

You may have put a great deal of thought into becoming independent; it generally does not happen overnight. It is an important career move, brought about by the realization that in the current work environment no job is sacred or secure. Increasingly, corporations and companies are "reorganizing" (another term for "downsizing", that is, reducing the work force to cut costs, etc.) with employees working at jobs that may be here today and gone tomorrow.

THE ENTREPRENEURIAL PERSONALITY

The makeup of the successful entrepreneur is defined by a number of common characteristics. How do you measure up?

- Desire to be your own boss?
- Want to be master of your destiny?
- Have appropriate education and experience?
- Possess basic business skills?
- Have courage to move forward?
- Have inherited an entrepreneurial spirit?
- Have ability to be flexible in diverse work environments?
- Have the energy to persevere for long periods?
- Like working long hours?
- Like to travel and be away from home and family?
- Can afford to wait months before getting a pay check?
- Can afford to cover your own health care and business benefits, e.g., vacation?

If you answer "no" to three or four of the above questions, maybe you should spend more time thinking about going solo.

EXPERIENCE AND TRAINING

Do you have the necessary experience to become a successful independent coder? Most independents are paid by production, by the job, chart or piece. If you are a highly productive coder, capable of coding accurately and quickly, your earnings can be excellent. On the other hand, if you are on the slow side, you should carefully consider whether self-employment is the right career move for you. This is a production-driven service, and unless you are planning on creating a business where you will hire other people to work for you, your survival as an independent will depend on your skills as a quick and accurate coding specialist.

WHAT TO EXPECT

Many people have misconceptions about what it is like to be a self-employed health information consultant and think that is an easy way to "get rich" quick. When they approach me I generally ask: How much experience do you have? If you cannot respond positively to the question "Do you know what ICD-9 Codes are?" then you are surely not ready for independent coding. If you have been employed by physician offices or clinics and feel you are well qualified, you should concentrate your new coding business within your field of expertise.

Have you thought about a business plan and your target market? What clients do you expect to service? The fact is, unless you live in a large city, your clients may be few and far between. There will be a lot of traveling and, likely, added stress from driving in rush hour traffic. In

11

addition, you must consider the purchase of health, disability and liability insurance, and you will no longer be paid for your sick time or vacation.

Your pay check may be bigger, but remember, YOU have to pay your own taxes. (Tax obligations will be reviewed in another section of this book.) If you are not already gifted with all the skills necessary to operate your own independent business, you may have to hire consultants to do your bookkeeping, and you will have to purchase your own supplies, do your own billing and collecting, and perform a multitude of other responsibilities that go along with owning your own business.

You will need to keep up to date on accreditation processes and all applicable regulations as they apply to the different types of facilities where you consult. To do this you should join professional organizations and subscribe to various journals, attend seminars and network with others in your area of expertise.

To succeed, you will need to market yourself and your service professionally and consistently. You will have to develop your negotiating skills, offer excellent service at fees that are within the standard for your market area, and always be prepared for meetings with all necessary marketing materials and an up-to-date contract.

THE REWARDS OF SELF-EMPLOYMENT

Consulting is hard work, but there are many rewards to being self-employed. You are an adviser and an educator, your position allows you to meet and work with many people; you learn too, with each experience. Your work schedule is flexible and you are your own boss. You need not fear being laid off or being bothered with a boss who is constantly looking over your shoulder.

If you feel you can meet the demands we have discussed above — the professional qualifications and personal skills — then as a consultant you can provide a valuable service to health care facilities. And beyond that, you can achieve personal satisfaction and professional independence!

THE PROS AND CONS OF INDEPENDENT CONTRACTING

Thousands of people have chosen to become independent contractors. If you are considering practicing as an independent coder, first weigh the pros and cons:

PROS:
- You can schedule your work hours to suit your lifestyle.
- You will be relatively free from office/institutional politics and bureaucracy.
- You negotiate your own contract with each client and set your own fees.
- You assume a prestigious role in the health care community, and your working relations with other professionals may improve.
- You can tailor your benefits package to meet your own needs.
- You can take control of your own destiny.

CONS:
- You lose the security of continuous employment.
- You may experience strained working relations with professionals who feel threatened by your autonomy.

13

- You will compete for work with other independent coders.
- You will have to educate yourself about the financial and legal aspects of running a business, such as getting clients to pay their bills on a timely basis.
- You will have to carry the full responsibility for your liability.

MEDICAL CODING EDUCATION

"Learning is a lifelong adventure."

Coding is much more than just data entry. As health care continues to reform, one thing that will remain constant is the need for accurate coding. Coders will require a good deal of knowledge in anatomy and physiology (structure and function of the human body). This, along with pharmacology, will help you understand the information that is being reviewed and coded. Coders also need to educate themselves about the concept of managed care, which will require very skilled, accredited procedure coders.

However, if you are not a world class all-around coder, you needn't be discouraged about starting your own business. If you have done only outpatient surgery coding, start your contracting in that arena. Always remember that you are in the driver's seat. You decide what your limits are. Keep current on changing coding issues and always keep an open mind about expanding your coding skills.

Different health care facilities require different skill levels as well as different areas of expertise with each coder.

EDUCATION AND EXPERIENCE

Every successful career begins with a basic education, and coding is no exception. The experience you bring into the independent coding profession will be extremely helpful, and courses in the following will be necessary:

- High school diploma

- College course in anatomy and physiology

- Medical terminology

- Pharmacology, basic course

- Introduction to disease (It is very important to understand the disease process.)

- Completion of an accredited program for coding certification or an accredited health information medical record technology program. Certified Coding Specialist (CCS), Accredited Record Technician (ART), or Registered Record Administrator (RRA).

- Continuing education in health information management

You will need training and experience in the above areas in order to perform currently established professional coding job responsibilities.

JOB DESCRIPTION — CODER

The Health Information/Medical Record Technician/Coder codes information from the medical records of patients to generate a clinical patient care data base for the facility. The coder assures the accuracy of diagnostic and procedure statistics for the facility as well as optimizes appropriate reimbursement by the timely coding of diagnoses and procedures using the required classification systems.

SPECIFIC RESPONSIBILITIES

- The coder reviews and screens the entire medical record to abstract medical, surgical, laboratory, pharmaceutical, demographic, social and administrative data from the medical record in a timely manner.

- The coder identifies and sequences appropriately all diagnoses and procedures that may impact the facility's reimbursement, by doing so in an accurate and ethical manner for optimum reimbursement while maintaining a balance in quality and quantity.

- Often, the coder is required to consult with the physician for clarification of clinical data.

- The coder must keep abreast of regulatory changes affecting coded information required by the Health Care Financing Administration (HCFA) and other regulating bodies and third party reimbursement regulators. This can be done through continuing education.

17

- The coder maintains knowledge of current information related to third party reimbursement regulations and seeks continuing education in all phases of coding acumen.

- The coder achieves a balance in quality and quantity with a goal of maintaining both elements at a prescribed level of efficiency.

- The coder abides by AHIMA's established code of ethical principles to safeguard the public and contribute within the scope of the profession to quality and efficiency in health care, thus promoting ethical conduct.

OTHER POTENTIAL DUTIES/RESPONSIBILITIES

- Assigns Diagnostic Related Groups (DRGs) after identifying not only the principal diagnosis (reason for admission) but also significant complications and/or comorbidities as well as operating room procedures following comparison of relative weights in the DRG Grouper software, and selection of the highest reimbursement allowable among alternative principal diagnoses documented in the record.

- Identifies and abstracts information from medical records for special studies and audits, internal and external.

TECHNICAL SKILLS REQUIRED

To be a successful coding specialist, you must master numerous technical skills.

- Experience with and knowledge of instructional notations and conventions of ICD-9-CM and CPT/HCPCS classification systems and the ability to follow detailed guidelines related to their use in assigning single and sequencing multiple diagnosis and procedure codes for appropriate reimbursement and data collection.

- Ability to read handwritten and transcribed documents in the medical record, interpret information and enter complete and accurate data into an on-line computer system.

- Comprehensive knowledge of medical diagnostic and procedural terminology.

- College level understanding of disease processes, anatomy and physiology, necessary for assigning accurate numeric and alphanumeric codes.

- Knowledge of federal, state and local government regulations and requirements which pertain to patient care information.

- Knowledge of legalities and confidentiality issues involved with release of clinical or billing information.

- Knowledge of third party payer reimbursement requirements and an understanding of relative values for multi-medical specialties, encounters, and procedures in acute care and ambulatory care settings.

DECISION-MAKING AND RESEARCH SKILLS

- Ability to query, analyze and determine the type of data needed to meet the request for information.

- Ability to communicate technical and clinical information concerning patient care and classification systems at different levels.

- Ability to apply policies and procedures regarding data security and confidentiality to protect the inappropriate release of information.

INTERPERSONAL AND ORGANIZATION SKILLS

- Communicates effectively, orally and in writing with physicians and peers.

- Communicates medical information with consideration of ethical and professional standards.

- Upholds standards of confidentiality regarding patients and physicians.

- Remains current with periodic updates of all coding manuals and guidelines.

- Has ability to manage time schedules, deadlines, multiple requests and priorities and to maintain productivity.

"As health care continues to reform, one thing that will remain constant is the need for accurate coding, which is much more than just data entry."

BUSINESS AND MANAGEMENT SEMINARS

There are many useful resources that offer seminars and workshops to enhance personal, professional and coding skills. Here are some examples:

Basic ICD-9 CM
Intermediate ICD-9-CM
DRG Basics
Advanced ICD-9-CM and DRG Update
Basic CPT — the yearly CPT changes
Outpatient and Emergency Room Coding

Don't forget technology and self-improvement workshops such as the examples below:

- Prioritizing Your Time
- Supervising People
- Conflict Resolution and Confrontation Skills
- Project Management
- Business Writing for Results
- Business Writing for Busy Professionals
- Microsoft Office
- Building Your Skills in Excel
- Using and Understanding Windows
- Tips & Techniques for Increasing Productivity
- Troubleshooting/Maintenance of IBM/PCs & Compatibles
- Stress Management
- How to Manage Conflict, Anger & Emotion
- Communication Skills for Women
- How to Achieve Exceptional Customer Service
- The Internet
- The Grammar & Usage Seminar

- How to Develop and Administer a Budget
- How to Manage Multiple Projects, Meet Deadlines & Achieve Objectives
- Coaching Skills for Managers & Supervisors
- Management Problems of the Technical Person in a Leadership Role
- Handling Employee Discipline & Performance Mistakes
- How to Deal with Negative People

ORGANIZATIONS OFFERING SEMINARS

J. A. Holloway & Associates, Inc.
800-888-4966

Seminars International
800-843-8084

CareerTrack
800-334-6780
http://www.careertrack.com

Cabot Marsh (a Quadrimed company)
40 Bethlehem Plaza
Bethlehem, PA 18018
800-373-5620
Fax 610-882-1796
E-mail: cabotmkt@cabotmarsh.com

Fred Pryor Seminars
800-255-6139
(catalog of seminars, tapes and books available)

SkillPath Seminars
800-873-7545
E-mail: skillpath@mcimail.com
or 729372@mcimail.com

Opus Communications
800-650-6787
http://www.opuscomm.com
E-mail: customer-service@opuscomm.com

National Seminars Group
800-258-7246
http://www.natsem.com

CREDENTIALS AVAILABLE

- Accredited Record Technician (ART)

- Registered Record Administration (RRA)

- AHIMA Certified Coding Specialist (CCS)

- AHIMA — Certified Coding Specialist — Physician Based Credential (CCS-P). This certification was introduced to provide a professional certification for physician-based coders as a result of the increased movement of health care industry resources from the inpatient to the outpatient setting. CCS-P examination is recommended for, but not limited to, physician-based coders with three or more years experience in the field.

For CCS-P and CCS certification guidelines, which include overviews of competencies necessary to pass the examinations as well as logistical information, contact Applied Measurement Professionals Inc., 913-541-0400.

- •AAPC (American Academy of Procedural Coders). This is the largest professional network of CPT coders in the nation. The AAPC provides two national accreditation programs for physician service and outpatient facility procedural coders: (CPC) Certified Procedural Coder and (CPC-H) Certified Procedural Coder — Hospital. There is AAPC Independent Study Program available.

For information contact:

American Academy of Procedural Coders
2144 South Highland Drive, Suite 100
Salt Lake City, Utah 84106
800-626-CODE; Fax 801-485-7803
Coding Hotline 900-555-CODE

There is a wide variety of coding workshops available from Basic ICD-9-CM to Advanced ICD-9-CM-DRG Coding; basic CPT to advanced CPT coding and HCPCS coding. Subscribe to some of the publications such as *Advance* and *For the Record* for information on availability and location of these workshops. Also, state and regional health care organizations will provide you with information on workshops available near you.

CONTINUING PROFESSIONAL EDUCATION

"Education, through which we grow and mature,
should be a continuing life goal."

As an independent coder you will find it very useful to belong to as many professional organizations as possible, such as AHIMA (American Health Information Management Association, 312-787-2672), state/regional associations, and coding roundtables. These groups will provide you with valuable literature and mailings. Having access to coding reference manuals, Coding Clinic, DRG update pamphlets and other items is essential in the success of your coding business. Keeping up with coding changes is vital to your survival. (Refer to the References/Resources that we have provided in the appendix of this book).

KNOWLEDGE IS POWER

Coding is one aspect of medical record practice that demands background in medical science and clinical technology. The work of coding entails a translation of diagnostic and procedure information into a classification system. Translation involves knowledge of two languages. The coder must know the two languages of medical/clinical knowledge and the ICD-9-CM classification system. It is essential that the coder understand clinical knowledge in a basic way in order to do an adequate job of translating the pertinent information in the medical record to the ICD-9 classification system.

Most coders received knowledge in medical science and clinical technology during their education process, either in ART/RRA programs or in coding certification courses. However, the educational portions of their training in clinical knowledge are very basic and brief, and most coders do not know everything they need to know about medicine upon graduation from their medical record programs. Most of the information needed by coders is obtained through on-the-job experience. Continuing education programs in clinical knowledge can assist the coder greatly in building the knowledge base so important to his or her coding work.

WORKSHOPS AND SEMINARS

Workshops and seminars are some of the most powerful self-improvement and professional development tools available today. Spending time in a stimulating, idea-filled environment is a motivating experience and a great place to network. These events can be excellent professional opportunities, especially when you plan ahead.

Every conference you attend provides an opportunity to meet and get acquainted with your colleagues, learn about their businesses and accomplishments, and share mutual concerns. It is important to get to know the conference participants. And be prepared to LISTEN. Meet as many people as possible, exchange business cards, and establish a personal network that you will be able to use in the future. It will prove invaluable.

Get to know the conference leaders. These individuals expect participants to speak with them informally during the conference breaks and appreciate your interest in conference subject matter as well as your well-thought-out questions and comments. Don't hesitate to explore specific topics in more depth with speakers. You will find them generally eager to share their wealth of information on the topics they present. The increased knowledge and myriad ideas you bring back from conferences will enhance your skills, and if you exercise these skills, your seminar experience will pay dividends to you in the months and years to come.

CODING ROUNDTABLES

In July 1992 the Society for Clinical Coding was formed to provide a forum for practitioners specializing in the coding of health care data, contribute to the education of all coders, promote the recruitment of new coders, build and enhance alliances, and advance the quality of coded data. Currently, the society is represented by more than 2,000 coding and data quality professionals. The society addresses both ICD-9-CM and CPT coding in all health care settings.

Coding roundtables have been established to discuss coding issues and to provide comprehensive reference guides for coding resources and educational sessions. The society and roundtables also offer coders opportunities to keep on top of current coding issues, network with peers, and make contact with prospective clients. For information about the Society for Clinical Coding and upcoming workshops, contact 800-670-2760 or www.ahima.org.

KEEPING UP WITH TECHNOLOGY AND TRENDS

To provide accurate services, it is essential for the coder to keep up with new technology in medicine. Medical science changes very rapidly, and participation in clinical knowledge seminars is essential for continuing education.

As an independent coding contractor, keep a sharp eye on health care reimbursement trends as it will be very important to your business success. Coders must stay current and code to the highest level of specificity. Education about the DRG system will be a #1 priority for your background needs. If it is an area where your coding skill level is weak, immediately begin to learn about these coding tools.

Evaluate your resources:

> **Coding Materials** — Get the most current copy of CPT. This will need to be updated every year. (ICD-9 is updated October 1st every year.)

> **Coding Expertise** — Attend inservice or seminars on CPT coding.

KEEPING CURRENT ON CODING UPDATES

To maintain your skills and credibility as a coder, it is important for you to stay current and be thoroughly knowledgeable about AHA's *Coding Clinic*, which is published four times a year. *Coding Clinic* sets and clarifies coding guidelines and is a invaluable resource. Once coding guidelines are published, coders are responsible for following them. Currently, there are guidelines for inpatient, outpatient and physician office codes.

Mark a set time on your calendar when you will routinely review your updates as follows:

- Review *AHA Coding Clinic Quarterly*
- Training and Development
- Review yearly CPT and HCPCS coding changes

It takes effort to keep current on industry codes and trends, but you will find it well worth the time and energy expended. By knowing the coding field thoroughly, you will be able to work more efficiently, accurately, and confidently.

BECOMING CREDENTIALED

"Certification demonstrates professional competence."

The purpose of any certification is to demonstrate that certain standards of practice have been achieved. On June 13, 1992, the American Health Information Management Association (AHIMA) administered the first certification examination for medical record coding specialists. The first Certified Coding Specialist (CCS) credential was awarded to 1600-plus individuals who passed the examination. In offering the CCS, AHIMA hopes to see the quality of coding improve and thus the accuracy of coded data enhanced.

- •The Certified Coding Specialist credential is intended to provide recognition to those who have coding skills beyond entry level, ultimately increasing coding manpower and providing a career ladder for coders. The demographics of the survey indicated that of all candidates credentialed one-third were credentialed as RRAs or ARTs, the remaining two-thirds either had other credentials such as RN, CRT, CPHQ, CMT, or no credential.

●The Certified Coding Specialist - Physician Based (CCS-P) credential was introduced in 1997 by AHIMA to provide professional certification for physician-based coders and to increase coder expertise in physician-based ICD-9-CM, CPT and HCPCS Level II medical record coding. For CCS-P and CCS certification guidelines, which include overviews of competencies necessary to pass the examinations as well as logistical information, contact Applied Measurement Professionals Inc., 913-541-0400.

Because of the increased movement of the health care industry resources from the inpatient to the outpatient setting, the CCS-P examination is recommended for but is not limited to physician-based coders with three or more years experience in the field of physician office coding.

If you are not already a credentialed coder, consider this for a future goal. The examination is recommended for coders experienced in hospital inpatient (ICD-9-CM) and ambulatory care, and CPT-HCPCS medical record coding. It is hoped that the CCS examination will serve to promulgate uniform national coding guidelines and standards of excellence in coding.

In order for a CCS and CCS-P to maintain certification there is a mandatory self-assessment once a year and an annual maintenance-of-certification fee. A small number of educational programs exclusively for coding currently exist. Contact AHIMA for a directory of programs available.

> *Although membership in professional organizations is recommended, a coder does not have to belong to coding associations to become certified or to maintain certification status.*

Resolution

Topic: Improving the Quality of Healthcare Data

Intent: Advance data quality management by encouraging AHIMA members to take leadership roles in this area.

Addressed to: All HIM professionals and AHIMA's strategic partners

Originator: AHIMA Data Quality Management Task Force

Approved by: 1997 House of Delegates

Whereas, integrated delivery and managed care give rise to new demands for information and use of new information technologies;

Whereas, ever-changing healthcare industry trends impact all aspects of data quality management including practice venues, roles, requisite skills, and knowledge;

Whereas, AHIMA's Board of Directors identified data quality management as a future HIM role;

Whereas, AHIMA will continue to clarify and define data quality management roles;

Whereas, work on data quality management as a Vision 2006 role is now under way and early planning demonstrates that success will require Association-wide commitment;

Whereas, ultimate success depends on the willingness of individual members to be responsible for preparing for new data quality management roles by acquiring new knowledge and skills;

Whereas, AHIMA and its members are resourceful and committed; and

Whereas, AHIMA and its members have a history of successfully adapting to change and taking advantage of new opportunities; therefore, be it

Resolved, That AHIMA educate members and students to develop management techniques for each component of data quality measurement and management; and

Resolved, That AHIMA and its component organizations promote the value of data quality management, participate in national initiatives to improve data quality measurement and management through standards, classification systems, education, and other efforts and assume leadership roles to ensure that the HIM profession continues to play a pivotal role in data quality management.

For guidelines for both the CCS-P and the CCS certifications or for an application and/or status report, contact AHIMA at the address below. AHIMA's guidelines include overviews of the competencies necessary to pass the CCS-P and CCS certification examinations, and AHIMA can also send you information about times and locations of examinations.

Candidate Services Department
Attention: AHIMA Examination
Applied Measurement Professionals, ICC
8310 Nieman Road
Lenera, KS 66214-1579
913-541-0400, Extremity. 450
Fax 913-541-0156

For examination content contact:

AHIMA (American Health Information Management Association)
Attention: CCS/CCS-P Examination
919 N. Michigan Ave., Ste. 1400
Chicago, Il 60611-1683
312-787-2672
Fax 312-787-5926

CERTIFICATION

Certification is a personal choice for the health care coder. Although the requirements for certification may vary from institution to institution, it is increasingly in demand for inpatient coders.

CERTIFICATION ORGANIZATIONS FOR THE OUTPATIENT CODING SPECIALIST

There are opportunities to become certified/credentialed in the outpatient coding arena.

American Academy of Procedural Coders (AAPC): This is the largest professional network of CPT Coders.

American Guild of Patient Account Managers (AGPAM): A coding certification which is becoming more and more widely accepted.

American Health Information Management Association (AHIMA): CCS-P (Certified Coding Specialist - Physician Based)

Medical Group Managers Association (MGMA): A very intensive coding course (based in Utah).

> *NOTE: A coder does not have to belong to a professional organization to become certified or to maintain certification status. However, professional organizations can provide many opportunities and resources that will aid the coder in maintaining continuing education credits (CECs) for ongoing certification.*

MEDICAL TRANSCRIPTIONISTS AS CODERS

*"Medical coding is a viable career alternative for
skilled medical transcriptionists."*

What is medical transcription? Medical transcription is the translation of medical dictation into accurate information of a patient's care and treatment in the health care record. Medical transcriptionists are medical language specialists, and the reports they produce are indispensable to modern health care. All health care providers face increasing pressures to provide quality patient care as quickly as possible, documented by ever-more-thorough records. To meet these needs, well trained transcriptionists are in great demand for accurate recording of patient care and treatment. Coding specialists rely on these accurately transcribed documents to review and determine what care and procedures are to be coded in the health care record.

Skilled medical transcriptionists have a broad understanding of medical science and clinical technology and are able to produce more accurate work because they have a basic understanding of medical procedures and patient care. While transcribing, a well-trained transcriptionist has a mental picture of the concept or the process that is the focus of dictation. And when a physician garbles dictation or uses a sentence structure that is not clear, the transcriptionist often relies on her or his knowledge base to transcribe with accuracy and meaning. In many ways the background education of the medical transcriptionist parallels that of the health care coder in that both must have knowledge in the following areas:

- Medical terminology
- Anatomy and physiology
- Computer skills/keyboarding
- Ability to work independently with little or no supervision
- Ability to understand/use appropriate reference materials.

Many medical transcriptionists become certified. The certification examination covers areas in medical terminology, English language usage, anatomy and physiology, disease processes, health care record and professional development, as well as a test transcription of original dictation. The most widely recognized certification is through the Medical Transcription Certification Program.

To request information about the certification program contact MTCP.

MTCP
209-551-0833
Fax 209-551-1722

Medical transcriptionists can adapt their professional knowledge base to cross over into other fields of health care, and coding is a very viable alternative or supplemental career path. Given the self-discipline, skills and knowledge of anatomy, physiology, medical terminology that medical transcriptionists bring into the coding arena, it is not surprising that many master the new field's requirements quickly and easily and become excellent coders.

Independent medical transcriptionists who expand their careers into coding have an advantage as they have already been working as home-based independents. Their businesses are established and they possess some understanding of coding concepts. For those who are already established in the medical transcription industry, some additional training in coding will give them another marketable skill.

Adding ICD-9 codes at the time of medical transcription is valuable. Including diagnostic codes at the time of transcription saves a step and gives transcriptionists another service to offer. Many transcription and coding services are offering both benefits: coding services are offering to transcribe discharge summaries, and transcription services are offering to code the reports that they transcribe.

Caution here: Discharge summaries may be inadequate (at times providing only one diagnosis) and incomplete for coding purposes.

BIOGRAPHY OF A SUCCESSFUL INDEPENDENT CODING/BILLING/RECOVERY SPECIALIST

Mary L. Smith, owner/operator of Advanced Billing Concepts, began her career in health care as a medical transcriptionist for a large medical group in Modesto, California. She worked several years in a clinic in the medical transcription department and then moved on to a home-based setting as a medical transcriptionist.

Several years later Mary and her family relocated to the Lake Tahoe area where she took a position in a large clinic as a medical transcriptionist. She was fortunate to work for an employer who promoted professional- as well as self-improvement. She was given the opportunity to expand in the coding and billing arena, and the clinic allowed her as much opportunity for education as she felt she needed. She attended coding classes, seminars, acquired an abundance of reference materials and was able to move into the coding/billing position. She went on to provide coding services to other practices in the area and soon found herself working full time in the coding/billing field.

BENEFITS OF A MEDICAL TRANSCRIPTION BACKGROUND

Mary Smith is convinced that her background in medical transcription, through which she became proficient in anatomy/physiology and medical terminology, helped her immensely in transitioning into coding and billing. With her thorough knowledge of medical transcription terminology and her familiarity with the body systems, she was able to understand what physicians were talking about when she first began coding. Mary states that this made all the difference in the world. In addition, she enjoyed another bonus derived from her transcription experience — familiarity with report formats and knowing where to look for specific information she needed to complete the coding and billing procedures.

NETWORKING-ADVERTISING

One of the best resources for coding information is AHIMA (American Health Information Management Association), and we recommend that you join this organization. This membership entitles you to membership in most state/regional associations at no extra charge. As a member you will have the opportunity to network with your peers at professional meetings and conventions and seminars and have access to journals, newsletters and other publications that provide valuable references for coders and other health care professionals.

INTERNET RESOURCES — "NET" WORKING

"Networking is a necessity for today's health care professional."

The June 1998 edition of *Advance, for Health Care Professionals* published the 1998 Annual HIMSS Leadership Survey conducted by the Health Care Information Management Systems Society (HIMSS) in which 93% of conference attendees (1380) responded. A significant 95% of the respondents reported that their organizations use the Internet. This was an increase from 87% reported in 1997. Twenty-nine percent of respondents also reported that their organizations have an *intranet* (interlink between all facilities within an organization) available to all employees. This is compared to 6% recorded in 1997.

Become familiar with on-line services and the Internet if you haven't already. It is a great resource for networking. There are many health care Web sites, organization Web sites and newsgroups. To help you weave through the various Web sites, we recommend *NetPractice, A*

Beginner's Guide to Healthcare Networking on the Internet, by Mary Frances Miller. It is a self-instructional, practical guide that assumes you know nothing about the Internet, and is very easy to follow.

Contact **Opus Communications** at 617-639-1872/Fax 617-639-2982, or E-mail: customer_service@opuscomm.com. Visit their Web site http://www.opuscomm.com.

A new feature added by *Advance for HIM Professionals* is a CCS Prep now on the Internet. This is a Web site to help individuals prepare for the CCS and CCS-P exams. Each installment on the Web includes quizzes, questions and answers found on the Web site: www.advanceweb.com.

If you are not online, contact *Advance* at the following address:

Advance
650 Park Avenue, Box 61556
King of Prussia, PA 19406-0956
800-355-5627, ext. 149
610-265-8293
E-mail: HIMEDIT@merion.com

> *NOTE: We have referred to several Web sites in this book, however, Web pages are like paid advertisements and can come and go with time. It is impossible to guarantee that the resources that are referred to at the time of this writing will still be available online in the future.*

RULES OF THE NET

The World Wide Web has made it relatively easy for people to access information, and medical data (including communicating with physicians) is a hot item. Unfortunately, there is a lack of anonymity associated with online use and there are individuals who have found ways to monitor Web sites and chat rooms and, in some cases, information swapping is a hot black marketing item. Online privacy is an issue that is being debated in Washington, and through Federal Trade Commission (FTC) hearings. With the government's involvement in the online privacy issue, there may be some legislation coming down the pike, but no one knows if it will be adequate. Technology changes so rapidly that by the time a mechanism is implemented, something new will probably be in place.

CONFIDENTIALITY ON THE INTERNET

The American Health Information Management Association (AHIMA) is an active participant in the issues surrounding online privacy and has developed its own guidelines for online privacy. To review the official position of AHIMA and MTIA (American Health Information Management Associating and Medical Transcription Industry Alliance) on the issue of "Confidential Health Information and the Internet," refer to the appendix of this book.

Here are some basic rules of "netiquette" (Internet behavior and ethics) to keep in mind before going online:

- •Never give your user ID or password to another person.
- •Never assume your e-mail messages are private. Never send something that you would mind seeing on the evening news.
- •Keep paragraphs and messages short and to the point.
- •When quoting another person, edit out whatever isn't directly applicable to your replay. Nobody likes reading a long message in quotes for the third or fourth time, only to be followed by a one line response. "Yeah, me too."

- Focus on one subject per message.
- Include your signature at the bottom of e-mail messages.
- Capitalize words only to highlight an important point. Capitalizing whole words that are not titles is generally termed as SHOUTING!
- Never send chain letters through the Internet. Sending them can cause the loss of your access.
- Be professional and careful what you say about others. E-mail is easily forwarded.
- Cite all quotes, references and sources and respect copyright and license agreements. Be careful when using sarcasm and humor. Without face-to-face communications your joke may be viewed as criticism.

Some good resources on netiquette can be found via the Internet by typing the keyword "netiquette."

The Net: User Guidelines and Netiquette by Arlene H. Rinaldi

Netiquette: Core Rules of Netiquette by Virginia Shea

Questions About Netiquette

… and there are more.

Remember to think about the impact your messages might have on others. Discuss positions rather than personalities. Adhere to the same standards of courteous behavior when you are online as when you are offline. Remember, although you are using the computer to communicate, you are still communicating with human beings.

TYPES OF CODING SYSTEMS

"Medical coding systems are complex because the human body is fearfully and wonderfully made."

What is ICD-9-CM? ICD stands for the International Classification of Diseases (1975 Revision, World Health Organization). The ICD-9 was published in Geneva, Switzerland in 1977. The ninth revision, Clinical Modification (ICD-9-CM), was first published in 1978 by the Commission on Professional and Hospital Activities (CPHA). A second printing providing guidelines for fifth-digit codes was released by CPHA in March 1980 and September 1980. This version was also released by the United States Department of Health and Human Services (DHHS). The purpose of these publications is to provide a uniform coding system to facilitate the study of diseases in both statistical and clinical applications.

As this book is being written, the new ICD-10-CM is currently in the works, and we expect medical coding specialists will be working with it soon.

INTERPRETING CODING WITH ICD-9-CM

Using ICD-9-CM is comparable to using a different language. It is a language of assigned numbers which have very specific meanings. As with any language, there are rules of grammar and usage, required elements, conventions, and certain prohibitions which are recognized, accepted and understood by both the originator and the recipient. Therefore, consider ICD-9-CM as a tool of communication, i.e., a language. Physicians are expert in the language of medicine; however, they do not speak ICD-9-CM. They become frustrated with the coding system. Correct coding is the result of a cooperative effort between the physician and the professional coder.

Using ICD-9-CM, the definition "diseases" is very broad. The term "disease condition" includes injuries, conditions of maternity, newborn infants, symptoms, and encounters with the health system for reasons other than the treatment of diseases, e.g., physicals, counseling, etc.

To code using the ICD-9-CM you must have had some educational training or experience in a medical records department and be familiar with medical terminology. Knowledge of anatomy and physiology is essential and an introduction to disease classifications is almost as important. If you are not acquainted with medical terms, you may need to go more slowly in places, consult a medical dictionary, and have an anatomy reference handy. You won't remember everything you learned in anatomy class so be sure to keep your anatomy book handy. Pharmaceutical, laboratory, and pathology medical references are also recommended.

To correctly use a complex system which was originally designed for the collection of data for research, not as part of a billing system, requires that the coder be professionally trained. This will entail enrolling in a coding course, attending continuing education seminars, and subscribing to professional publications which bring the latest information, including newly developed codes.

THE EMERGENCE OF ICD-10

In the United States a coding classification system must meet multiple needs, including reimbursement, patient care data bases, longitudinal record systems, public health statistics and research, monitoring of utilization and quality of care. The ICD-10 system by HCFA will emerge in the near future, targeted for the year 2000. It is not too soon to begin to plan for the conversion. At this writing the ICD-10 Procedure Coding System is being tested, and final revisions should be completed in the near future.

HCFA and the National Center for Health Statistics have agreed that ICD-10-PC2 will be implemented concurrently with the ICD-10-CM Diagnostic Coding System (now being developed) to minimize impact on users of this new system.

The Purpose of the new Inpatient Coding System is to provide more reliable and precise coding, which should facilitate payment and provide more precise statistics for reports and studies.

With the emergence of ICD-10, even the best coders will require a considerable amount of training. Training sessions will be available through AHIMA via satellite conferencing, videotapes and seminars.

There will be far reaching information system and product development/planning changes in the current coding system. Major information system issues include a new DRG grouper program, medical record abstracting and patient accounting/billing systems that will need to be revised to accommodate the new alphanumeric coding scheme.

Coding policies and procedures will require updating, followed by staff education and communication of revisions; clinical data documenters such as physicians, nurses, therapists., etc. and clinical data information users such as managers, planners and administration will need to be educated about the biases and limitations inherent in the new coding system.

The new coding system is now in its third year of development and nearing completion of the ICD-10 Procedure Coding System (PCS). The new system for coding procedures (inpatient) will replace Volume 3, the Procedures Classification, of the current ICD-9-CM. Under a contract with the Health Care Financing Administration (HCFA), 3-M Health Information Systems is heading up the new project.

THE HCPCS CODING SYSTEM

HCPCS (pronounced "hick-picks") is an acronym for HCFA (Health Care Financing Administration) Common Procedure Coding System. The system was developed in 1983 by the Health Care Financing Administration (HCFA) for the purpose of standardizing the coding systems used to process Medicare claims on a national basis. HCPCS codes must be used when billing Medicare carriers and in some state Medicaid carriers.

The HCPCS coding system is a three-level system consisting of CPT (Level I), National (Level II) and Local (Level III) codes. These codes are revised annually and you will need to obtain a copy of the revised codes each year.

There is a general lack of knowledge and understanding about exactly how and when to use the HCPCS codes instead of CPT. However, this presents a new opportunity for contract coders (independents), and your education in these areas will help expand the market demand for your business.

WHY USE HCPCS?

HCFA mandates use of HCPCS codes on Medicare claims and many state Medicaid offices also require their use.

Level I — CPT

This is the American Medical Association's CPT (Physicians' Current Procedural Terminology), developed and maintained by the AMA. CPT lists five-digit codes with descriptive terms for reporting services performed by healthcare providers. It is the country's most widely accepted coding reference. CPT was first published in 1966 and is updated annually.

Level II — HCPCS/National Codes

Because CPT does not contain all the codes needed to report medical services and supplies, HCFA developed a second level of codes (Level II). These codes are grouped by the type of service or supply they represent and are updated annually by HCFA. HCPCS/National codes are now required for reporting most medical services and supplies provided to Medicare and Medicaid patients. An increasing number of private insurance carriers are also encouraging or requiring these codes.

Level III — Local Codes

The third level contains codes assigned and maintained by individual state Medicare carriers. It is important to note that the difference in these codes is that they are not common to all carriers.

Individual carriers assign these codes to describe new procedures that are not yet available in Levels I or II. They are often introduced on an as-needed basis throughout the year. It is important to keep up to date on the information received from the individual carriers regarding the use of these local codes.

CPT CODING

CPT stands for *Current Procedural Terminology, 4th Edition*, commonly known as CPT-4, a listing of descriptive terms and identifying codes for reporting medical services and procedures performed by physicians and other medical professionals. CPT codes first appeared in 1966 and were developed for the purpose of providing uniform language to accurately describe medical, surgical and diagnostic services, and to provide an effective means of reliable nationwide communication among physicians, patients and third party payers. CPT codes serve the same variety of important functions as the ICD-9 codes. A thorough understanding of CPT is critical to reimbursement. Medicare and Medicaid programs require the use of CPT codes, and most commercial insurance carriers also use CPT codes.

As new procedures are developed, old procedures become obsolete. Existing procedures are modified to reflect changes in medical practice. It is for this reason that the American Medical Association revises and publishes CPT on an annual basis.

CPT IS HERE TO STAY

Coding for ambulatory procedures has improved since the use of CPT-4, and understanding what CPT-4 is all about helps improve outpatient coding skills. Here are some basics for coding in the outpatient setting:

- Read and analyze the operative report carefully and comprehensively.
- Do not code from the physician's procedural statement only.
- Use as many codes as necessary to describe what was actually done.
- Read the complete narrative description of each code. Don't pick the first code that looks good to you.
- Read all explanatory notes. Don't select a code without knowing its correct use.
- Know documentation requirements for ambulatory surgery records and learn to recognize when you should demand more information from the surgeon or when you should insist on more documentation because you cannot accurately and completely code the procedure without it.

APGs — AROUND THE CORNER

Ambulatory Patient Groups (APGs) first came about after the OMNIBUS Budget Reconciliation Act (OBRA) of 1990 requiring that the Health Care Financing Administration (HCFA) develop and evaluate a Prospective Payment System (PPS) for the facility cost of outpatient care.

APGs are a patient classification system designed to be used as a basis for an outpatient PPS. APGs are for outpatient care the equivalent of Diagnostic Related Groups (DRGs) in the Medicare inpatient PPS.

The unit of payment selected for the APGs is the visit, whereas the payment for DRGs is the hospital's admission diagnosis with or without procedures. APGs recognize three types of visits: 1) the significant procedure visit, 2) the medical visit and 3) the ancillary visit.

In the near future, some form of outpatient PPS will become mandatory for all Medicare reimbursement, replacing cost-based reimbursement. The Balanced Budget Act of 1997 mandated that a Prospective Payment System for hospital-based outpatient care be implemented by January 1999. APGs are already in use as a Prospective Payment System for outpatient care in some states.

The health information management departments/coders need to prepare and educate themselves now for the implementation of APGs. The APG system will require accurate and consistent coding for all outpatient settings for appropriate reimbursement. There are useful references available for this purpose such as *St. Anthony's APG Source Book* and the *CPT Coding for Outpatient Surgery, HCPCS Report*.

EMERGING HELPFUL GUIDELINES

At this writing St. Anthony's Publishing has released a book that comprises official compliance documents to help professionals comply with government regulation and reduce the risk of false claims. The book is subtitled *"Official Guidelines for Inpatient and Outpatient Billing, Coding and Medical Documentation"* and is available through St. Anthony's Publishing (see resources in the back of this book).

For Medicare cases, in the absence of established guidelines, the PRO (peer review organization) has been empowered to develop guidelines for coding. This puts the PRO in the position of adversary, in some instances, when the established guideline does not necessarily reflect what the physician hospital or ASC (ambulatory surgery center) wants.

It is crucial that we as health care professionals take an aggressive, initiating stance in solving the mysteries of CPT-4 coding.

DIAGNOSTIC RELATED GROUPS (DRGs)

WHAT IS A DRG?

It is one of more than 500 groups that classify patients into clinical, cohesive groups that demonstrate similar use of hospital resources, procedures and length-of-stay patterns.

In 1983 the Federal Government (Congress mandated) established the Prospective Payment System (PPS), a system for payments for medical care on the basis of rates set in advance of the time period in which they apply. This unit of payment varies from individual medical services to broader categories.

The PPS designated standard prices for treatment of specific diagnosis related groups (DRGs) in Medicare patients.

WHERE DID THE DRG ORIGINATE?

The initial development of the DRG concept emerged in the late sixties at Yale University, where they were attempting to design a utilization management tool, not a payment plan. These were entries in a classification of types of hospitalizations based on groupings of diagnostic categories drawn from the International Classification of Diseases and modified by the presence of a surgical procedure, patient age, presence or absence of significant comorbidities or complications, and other relevant criteria.

In 1983 the federal government decided to utilize this concept to implement the diagnosis-related groups (DRGs), initially to create an effective framework for monitoring the quality and use of services in a hospital setting. The government mandated the use of DRGs in establishing payment amounts for individual admissions under Medicare's Prospective Hospital Payment System as required by the Social Security Amendments of 1983 (Public Law 98-21).

HOW IS A DRG ASSIGNED?

DRGs are assigned using the principal diagnoses and additional diagnoses (it is generally the first eight assignments that impact the DRG), the principal procedure and up to five additional procedure codes, age, sex and discharge status. One DRG is assigned to each inpatient stay. Diagnoses and procedures are designated by ICD-9-CM codes.

THE TYPICAL DECISION PROCESS USED TO ASSIGN A DRG TO A CASE

A case is assigned to one of 25 major diagnostic categories (MDC). Based on a principal diagnosis or operating room procedure, each MDC is organized into two sections: surgical or medical. The surgical section classifies all surgical conditions based upon operating room procedures. The medical section classifies all diagnostic conditions based upon diagnosis codes. MDCs are mutually exclusive and, in general, are organized by major body systems and/or associated with a particular medical specialty. Although the MDCs scope is too broad for clinical analysis it ensures that the DRG assignments are clinically coherent.

Further sorting of medical classification can be done by type of principal diagnosis and/or surgical classification by type of surgery. Finally, the case is analyzed for age and/or the presence of complications and comorbidities and assignment of a DRG is made. Complications and comorbidities are derived from ICD-9-CM diagnosis codes.

Each year, effective October 1 through September 30th, DRG assignments are adjusted based on relative weight, arithmetic mean length of stay, geographic means of stay and outliers thresholds.

Now coders play a key role in a hospital's financial health, working within the complex environment of the Prospective Payment System. In order to obtain an appropriate DRG assignment, coders must carefully review each medical record with DRG optimizing principles. Annually, new ICD-9-CM codes are also incorporated into the existing 500-plus DRGs and/or new DRGs added for that fiscal year.

HOW HOSPITALS ARE PAID VIA THE DRG SYSTEM

The DRG payment system is based on averages. That is, payment is determined by the resource needs of the average Medicare patient for a given set of diseases or disorders. These needs include the length of stay and the number and intensity of services provided. The more efficiently a provider delivers care, the greater its operating margin will be. Keys to a financially successful DRG program include the following:

- length of stay
- resource utilization (decreased numbers of tests and procedures)
- early discharge
- preadmission testing (increased use of)
- a comprehensive, legible, well-documented medical record, completed in a timely manner

Each DRG is assigned a relative weight by HCFA, and each hospital has a customized base rate designed to adjust payment, commensurate with the hospital's cost of providing services. DRG relative weight and a hospital's base weight are adjusted yearly, effective October 1st through September 30th, to reflect changes in health care resources consumption as well as economic factors. Payment is determined by multiplying the DRG relative weight by the hospital's base rate. The DRG with the highest relative weight is the highest paying DRG. Regardless of actual cost, the hospital receives **ONLY** the calculated payment.

Regarding the "Base Rate", DRGs are consistent. For example, for CHF (congestive heart failure) a weight factor of 1.01 is assigned. All hospitals are paid 1.01, but each hospital has a blended rate (base rate), which means that the hospital may get paid $4,000 for every one (1) point. This depends on several factors including the geographical location, economic climate, operating costs of the facility, local resources and coding history.

Besides reimbursement, the DRG has two major functions:

Evaluate the quality of care

- analyze treatment protocols, related conditions or demographic distribution (possible to do because all cases in a DRG are clinically similar)

58

- design critical pathways around DRGs
- launch benchmarking and outcome analysis using the DRG clinical framework
- confirm quality reviews to assess coding practices and physician documentation
- guide ongoing education of physicians, coders, and utilization review personnel

Evaluate the utilization of services

Each DRG represents the average resources needed in that DRG relative to the average resources needed by other DRGs. They can be used for the following:

- compare physician and departmental practice patterns and case-mix
- monitor complexity in relation to costs and utilization of services
- identify and monitor high volume conditions and services
- aid in forecasting future staff and facility requirements through DRG trend analysis

CASE MIX

Case mix is calculated to reflect relative cost of each hospital's mix of cases compared to the national average. The case mix index is calculated by HCFA (Health Care Financing Administration).

Under the DRG (coding) system, hospitals receive a flat payment per case based on the patient's diagnosis for services furnished to Medicare beneficiaries. Although a patient may be treated for several problems, the DRG payment is based on the principal diagnosis, or the condition determined to be chiefly responsible for the patient's admission to the hospital.

A federal DRG rate is set for both rural and urban hospitals in nine regions in the United States. These rates are updated annually. Regional adjustments are made to the labor-related portion of the national and regional payment rates to account for area differences in hospital wage levels. The dollar weight of a DRG is determined by a combination of a federally established dollar weight and the hospital's cost experience and history. Hospital-specific rates are computed by using the hospital's most recent cost report: base year costs/case mix index multiplied by the updating factor equals the hospital specific rate.

A low case mix may indicate unnecessary revenue loss. This information is important because health care facilities compile and analyze trending data, which is public information. Consultants can retrieve this information from a public network and target a facility that may be in need of special services because of a low case mix.

QUALITY CODING DATA

Since the adoption of DRGs in 1983, increased emphasis has been placed on coding to facilitate reimbursement. However, it is the responsibility of the coding professional to achieve and maintain quality coding data, regardless of the financial outcome. Ethics enter into every coding related function whether the coder is auditing for revenue enhancement and cost containment or coding daily discharges. Every coder should make a commitment to the coding industry's ethical standards and strive to achieve optimal performance while abiding by those standards .

REIMBURSEMENT SYSTEMS

Many reimbursement systems are code-based and utilize ICD-9-CM and/or CPT-4. They include the following:

- Ambulatory Patient Groups (APGs)

- Ambulatory Surgery Center (ASCs)

- Resource-Based Relative Value Scales (RBRVS)

There are several terms that define various reimbursement strategies and that state the use and purpose of coded data:

Maximize: Raise to highest degree possible

Minimize: Reduce to the least possible degree or amount

Optimize: Make the most of; develop or realize to the utmost extent; obtain the most efficient or optimum use of

It is the responsibility of the coder to ensure optimal reimbursement for the client. Maximizing, i.e., choosing an inappropriate principle diagnosis or "up-coding" a procedure to increase the DRG, is both unethical and illegal. This practice can EXPOSE the client AND the coder to fraud charges.

Minimizing, i.e., failing to comprehensively code all diagnoses and procedures supported by documentation and/or failing to sequence these codes correctly will result in lost reimbursement and a decrease in case mix for your client. This practice will cost you business so avoid doing it.

OPTIMIZE, OPTIMIZE, OPTIMIZE — WHAT YOU MUST DO TO BE SUCCESSFUL

Optimizing is the correct code assignment for, and sequencing of, **ALL** diagnoses and procedures supported by documentation. This requires both a thorough knowledge of the Prospective Payment System and the Coding Guidelines. This practice ensures the highest allowable reimbursement for your client. Optimization is what you, the coder, must do if you want to be successful.

The strategy for DRG optimization is as follows:

- Review the medical record for documentation to support a higher resource intensive diagnosis as principal diagnosis.
- Review the medical record for documentation of the procedures performed.
- Review the medical record to identify coexisting chronic conditions which have been exacerbated or required treatment with medications, or monitoring, or are a risk factor for the patient's treatment.
- Review the medical record to identify transient conditions which require treatment during the hospital stay.

Coding plays a significant role in determining future health care — from reimbursement to quality of care issues. It is crucial that coding functions be performed in accordance with ICD-9-CM and CPT-4 coding guidelines. This must be supported by accurate and timely physician documentation, which is essential in order for the coder to perform her or his function with integrity. Appropriate optimization allows for appropriate reimbursement.

In the future, accurate coding will be crucial to the development of new data systems which are based on the statistical information of the systems now in place.

ESTABLISHING YOUR INDEPENDENT CODING BUSINESS

*"The people who rain on your parade
usually don't have a parade of their own."*

You won't be the first independent coder, so be wise and gather as much information as you can from a variety of sources, including your competition. Learning the basic information, ways to be more efficient and how to avoid professional pitfalls from someone who has already been there will save you time, money and headaches. However, be cautious when opinions are offered. Good advice can be invaluable, but beware of naysayers with negative attitudes, who may never have taken a risk or were stymied by adverse experiences. Learn to differentiate fact from fantasy. Sit down and make a list of the benefits and drawbacks of being self-employed.

You are thinking "business" now. You need to plan for and take action regarding all aspects of organizing and running a business. That means developing your marketing strategy, your business operations strategy, and your financial strategy. You need to set goals and put systems in place to achieve those goals. You must make a personal commitment to work hard to achieve what you desire.

NEW INDEPENDENT FREEDOMS

Computer technology has opened new doors for coders, providing the option of working through networks, on-site or off-site, remote or home-based.

Freedom and mobility are givens for the independent entrepreneur, but you must have discipline to maintain that flexibility. Best of all, as an entrepreneur you have unlimited opportunity for success and fulfillment — as far as you want to go.

As an independent coder, you establish personal goals, set a schedule and manage daily life — you are in control!

ADVANTAGES OF SELF-EMPLOYMENT

Working as a coding consultant is generally challenging and sometimes exhausting, but there are also many rewards to being self-employed. You are an adviser and an educator, your position allows you to meet and work with many people; you learn, too, with each experience. Your work schedule is flexible and you are your own boss. You need not fear being laid off or being bothered by a boss who is constantly looking over your shoulder.

Once you have attained the appropriate professional qualifications and personal skills necessary to fulfill the requirements and responsibilities we have discussed above, you may begin your consulting career and enjoy the privilege of providing a valuable service to health care facilities. And beyond that, you can achieve personal satisfaction and professional independence!

STAYING FOCUSED

Being successful at your business will require that you remain focused, concentrating on individual projects over long periods of time.

While building your independent business you may need to forego vacations, sick days and weekend leisure. You may wear many hats and have numerous extra responsibilities — marketing, public relations, quality control, risk managing, bookkeeping, consulting. Simply stated, YOU are the business.

CONSULTING — THE PROS AND CONS

WHAT IS A CODING CONSULTANT?

A consultant is an adviser, a researcher, one who knows legalities and regulations. In coding, the following functions are typically performed by the coding consultant:

- Randomly review medical records, both concurrently and retrospectively.
- Reviews health information/medical record systems and procedures.
- Reviews previous visit reports to determine status of any problems, i.e., new problems, same problems, and recommends improvements.

•Prepares reports of findings, makes recommendations, and allows for discussion and feedback.

PROVIDING CONSULTING SERVICES TO OPTIMIZE DRGs

Providing outside consulting services to evaluate coding and DRG assignments done by in-house coders can be a very lucrative business. The financial impact a "less than optimum" DRG assignment can have on a hospital's cash flow and revenue may be significant. Many hospitals now contract with outside sources/consultants to evaluate coding and DRG assignments done by their medical records department coding staff.

Often, facilities lack time and resources to evaluate and educate in-house coders on an ongoing basis. By using outside consultants, hospitals can gain valuable coding and DRG education for their staff.

As a consultant you may review records. Some small hospitals will prefer 100% review of all discharges and all Medicare charts. Larger hospitals may specify a random sampling. The records should be reviewed within 60 days of discharge so there is time to rebill if there is money to be recovered.

Fees for this type consulting service may be based on a percentage of what is recovered for the facility in lost revenue; some companies charge a flat fee regardless of whether or not they recover any lost revenue.

As a consultant you may agree to provide educational feedback to the in-house coding staff. (Generally the facility will have the charts pulled for you.) You will also have to consider whether you want to provide services for outpatient coding.

BEING ETHICAL

When providing coding services, remember that at all times ethical standards apply. For instance, do not yield to the temptation to change the DRG for greater reimbursement for diagnoses that have no bearing on that current admission. Such an action would be unethical, and the PRO (peer review organization) might review your revision and reject it. Unethical practices expose you to the risks of reprimand, personal disgrace and a short-lived career as an independent coder. Choose a higher standard.

FRAUD AND ABUSE

Healthcare fraud and abuse is subject to high visibility among United States health care providers. Compliance planning will be on the immediate agenda for every health care organization.

As an independent coder, you must ensure that your coding practices are in compliance with legal and accepted professional standards.

- Follow AHIMA's official coding guidelines.
- Use the correct coding resources (CPT Assistant, Coding Clinic).
- Do not rely completely on computerized encoders. Make sure your coding books are readily accessible.
- Keep on top of all ICD-9-CM and CPT annual changes.
- Consider developing written coding policies and procedures for your home-based coding company.

POSITIONING YOURSELF IN THE CURRENT HEALTH CARE ENVIRONMENT

As coding specialists we are a profession of high achievers. We tend to be obsessive and compulsive about our work, frequently overcommit, have a problem saying "no" and knock ourselves out to be the best that we can be. We take pride in doing a great job. And, we like to control our work environment.

Some things cannot be totally controlled, however, and life and professions are always changing. Like many other industries, coding continues to evolve and will eventually go global. Right now the need for coding specialists is rapidly expanding into many new areas. This is good news, for as an independent coder you have opportunities to tap into resources that are in great need of your expertise. These include not only hospital inpatient/outpatient settings, but clinic settings, outpatient services, ambulatory care clinics, urgi-surgicenters, walk-in clinics, physician practices, skilled nursing facilities and many others.

At the present time, there are not enough "qualified" coding specialists to meet the demand, and there is tremendous need for education and training of support staff in medical care settings so that accurate coding and reimbursement can be implemented.

It is a very different playing field today than it was twenty years ago. Coding is now an industry, not simply a limited-use skill or profession. Furthermore, it is an industry in which opportunity abounds for independent coders ... at a time when thousands of workers are striving to homebase. This is no cottage industry. It is a revolution into independence. But each day holds a challenge and there are many changes yet to come. The biggest challenge is to remain competitive in today's marketplace.

HOW TO COMPETE SUCCESSFULLY

How do you position yourself to compete successfully in the global marketplace? Establish clear objectives that include vision, commitment and persistence. Be proactive in your plans for improving your business and your own professional development. Consistently and continuously work on your image and your service. Determine to excel, to be the best, and do it.

What professional image do you reflect? Your business image is every bit as critical to your success as are your coding specialist skills. Make your image a standout.

How will you market your services to potential clients? Establishing, operating, and growing your business is an ongoing process. Do you have a strategic plan for providing the best service? Ask yourself what is special about the service you provide your clients, and if you can't think of anything, improve your service. To compete in the marketplace effectively, your service must stand apart from your competitors. And in order for your business to remain competitive year after year, you should evaluate it at least biannually, determine weak areas, and immediately follow through on improvements.

What is your strategic plan if you lose a client? How will you cope if revenue declines? Experience has taught us that clients who are here today may be gone tomorrow. Have revenue replacement systems in place to carry you through those times when you may lose a client or revenue.

Continually seek out and research new industry trends that may affect the way in which you do your work. Be sure you have ready access to technical support in the event of unexpected equipment failure.

Keep your technology up to date so that your business will remain efficient and competitive.

Take responsibility as an independent business owner. Be accountable, consistent, reliable and qualified in the work that you commit to. Reflect a responsible, professional attitude in your personal image, the physical appearance of your office and how you present yourself to your clients. Your voice, eye contact and body language should always be positive and controlled. Your answering machine message, stationery and business cards should project a sense of excellence and professionalism.

Be consistent in your follow-through of projects. When business is slow, or when you're feeling low, continue to maintain a positive appearance.

Take advantage of downtime by doing quality audits of your work and focusing on details. Record audit logs and quality/productivity reports at designated times during each quarter cycle. With an open mind, consider the facts and determine if improvements are needed. Your self-audits may indicate you will benefit from improving your technical skills and knowledge base. Downtime is also a great opportunity to catch up on reading and industry trends, learn new business skills, and attend trade shows and workshops.

Be smart about your business investments. Cost containment is important. Avoid investing in equipment and technology that is just a "fad." Research the market. Don't run out and buy the latest and the greatest just so you can brag about it on the Internet or keep up with the Jones'. Carefully evaluate your options, network with others to see what is working for them. It's okay to step back for a time and see which way the tree is going to fall. Products are not always what they are touted to be, and the truest test is in the hands of users. Your safest bet is to go with a product that has been established in the marketplace and will suit the needs of your clients. For any product you are considering, investigate what technical support is available and make sure you have a backup in case of equipment failure.

Service is the name of the game these days. The current trend in coding — as well as in the business world generally — is toward service, service, and more service. For the greatest success, tailor your services to suit your client's needs, not yours. This is an area where you can stand out from others by offering your client excellent quality.

Market your services appropriately and adequately. Some coders target only their local market, which may be satisfactory for the moment but that market could change quickly. If there is a turnover in office personnel — office staff, office manager, medical director, or chief financial officer — a new employee with decision-making responsibility may decide not to use your services and/or to go with a larger service whose bid is lower than what you are charging. Suddenly, and perhaps with little prior notice, you may find yourself without a client. It is never wise to put all your eggs in one basket by targeting a too narrow market. This cannot be emphasized enough.

MAINTAINING YOUR COMPETITIVE EDGE

To remain competitive as a coding specialist, you should always work to improve your knowledge base, flexibility and diversity. To accomplish this, you will need to pursue continuing education, which is critically important, and always be prepared to adapt to changes in your work schedule. Peaks and valleys often occur in business and the coding business is no exception, so have a backup plan in place. In addition, the more diverse your talents as a coding specialist, the more valuable you will be to clients.

MAKING HEALTHY CHOICES

You have chosen to be a coding specialist, but if you dream of great success, you must make one more choice — to be the most qualified coding specialist you can be. At the present time, there is more coding work than there are qualified coding specialists. Do you feel threatened because you are under qualified? Or because you are not fully educated about what is going on in the coding industry's "big picture?" More choices await when you realize you can (and must!) take charge of your professional life.

Commit yourself to self-improvement and improve your knowledge base. Take that anatomy/physiology course, English grammar course, an advanced terminology course. Follow through on extra coding courses and invest in the latest up-to-date coding references. Attain a higher level of expertise not only in coding but in technology, because the more technically savvy will merit the higher pay. Learn everything you can about telecommuting to improve your position and scope in the market.

There are educational opportunities through local, state, regional and national programs. Membership is generally not a requirement for attendance. If you have minimal experience, network with other coders who telecommute. This is an area you should pursue and conquer. Limiting yourself to your little comfort zone may lead to your demise in the current global industry environment.

We still have choices. The future holds many opportunities. Even though coding is just one piece in the very complex health care puzzle, it is a very important piece. There are many avenues that we coders can pursue to expand our horizons and offer a diversity of services to our clients. For instance, coding that includes billing for services is a very viable option. It may be to your benefit to pursue this path.

There are challenging years ahead as we move into the 21st century. To reach our career potential during this time, we need to make healthy choices in our professional and personal lives. As health care coding specialists, we are in an excellent position to thrive and excel ... even during tough times. On occasion, we may need to remind ourselves that we chose this profession and must be willing to accept its challenges as well as its rewards. If we are to be players, we must play the game like champions, embracing change that moves us closer to the goal.

TYPES OF SERVICES TO OFFER

There are yet other areas where coders can provide significant support and consultation.

Hospital Coding: There is great demand for experienced hospital coders. Trade magazines and journals contain many ads calling for experienced medical record coders, coding consultants, medical coders, coder/analyst, etc. If you are a highly skilled coder, you can often "write your own ticket."

Medical Office Coding: As physician group practices increase, there will be an increase in the number of job opportunities for coders. It is difficult for stand-alone physicians to justify having a trained coder on staff, but in group practices there will be more opportunities to have trained expert coders. Stay alert for opportunities where you, an expert coder, can work teaching providers to correctly use the forms necessary for reimbursements.

73

Because coding directly influences reimbursement received, quality of coding is of foremost concern. One overlooked CC (complication or comorbid condition) can result in a loss of several hundred dollars. A missequenced principal diagnosis code or a forgotten procedure code may cost several thousand dollars in reimbursement.

Coding Audits: Coding accuracy checks (also known as "audits"), designed to catch coding errors, are viable options for any type health care facility, not just acute care hospitals. Although some facilities feel that the cost of performing coding accuracy checks is too costly, the elimination of only two or three major coding errors per month can offset the cost of such a contract.

BENEFITS/REVENUE RECOVERY

Many physician practices write off denied or reduced claims, believing that the reimbursement agency's decision is final with no recourse for the caregiver. Often, practices do not review their explanation of benefits (EOB) and are not even aware that a claim was "downcoded" or reduced. Reviewing is time-consuming for the practice, and office personnel sometimes lack the knowledge, skills and time to follow up these claims. However, routinely writing off claims, failing to review explanation of benefits, and failing to resubmit claims can be unnecessarily costly to a physician practice.

It is possible to recover lost revenue from denied or reduced claims by resubmitting the claim with corrected coding or additional documentation. A skilled coding specialist can review the EOB and help identify coding errors. These errors occur when carriers change codes and the notification of the change has passed by or been overlooked by office personnel, coding software updates have not been loaded onto the computer, or the initial code was incorrect.

As an independent coder, this is an area to consider for professional growth. Your coding consulting expertise would be extremely useful to the physician practice, and recovering lost revenue is a very lucrative way to expand your consulting business.

SKILLED NURSING FACILITY (SNF)

With growing pressures to contain health costs and improve quality management of health care, the unique expertise of the health information professional in data quality is needed to assure the accuracy of the requirements for data collection.

HOME HEALTH CARE AGENCIES

The home health care agency is another provider that codes for billing purposes. This could be another contract option for you. And, keep in mind their continuing needs for coding education as well.

Other settings that offer potential work for health information professionals include home care services, hospice care programs, correctional facilities, veterinary medicine settings and zoos!

AMBULANCE COMPANIES

Ambulance services code to bill for their services. Consider researching their needs for a possible coding contract.

> *"Recovering lost revenue is a very lucrative way to expand your consulting business."*

MANAGED CARE

Managed care will motivate large group practices to hire qualified coders.

As health information professionals/coders we can provide a valuable service to physicians and their personnel.

OUTPATIENT

Coding for the outpatient arena is a relatively easy way to get started in coding since all the information needed for coding is contained in just a few pages, in contrast to the inpatient setting where the entire record is needed to glean correct coding. Generally, CPT coding is used in outpatient work. You might consider a charge per report once you've determined how much time it takes you for each report coded.

THE WORK SITE — HOME-BASED CODING

As regulators mandate more coding data for all aspects of health care, hospitals, ambulatory care centers, clinics and physician practices are experiencing a backlog of charts to be coded. Employees are often located in cramped quarters or discover that there is no designated area for coding at all. Many hospitals have found a solution to this problem by home-basing their coder employees or contracting with home-based coding contractors.

Home-basing coding is possible in the new health care environment. As medical record information becomes available online, home-based coding is now a reality for independent coders. This area opens up wonderful business opportunities. Be well educated, organized and prepared to take advantage of these opportunities.

MEDICAL FACILITY BENEFITS OF HOME-BASED CODING

The results of utilizing home-based coders have been extremely positive, as has been the result of home-basing in the medical transcription industry. Production is increased, there are fewer interruptions, working conditions are improved and morale remains very high.

Hospitals have found that certain services can be coded entirely from the computer system, and as hospitals move toward the computerized patient record (see the chapter on the computerized patient record), online coding will come into its own.

Home-based coders can be either employees of the facility or contract workers. As employees, they may be paid on an incentive scale by the number of charts coded. In many cases there are no restrictions on the number of hours coders keep; they can work any time, day or night. (Independent coders may be paid by the record or on an hourly scale.)

Coders may work with paper copies of the records. These must be copied for the coders, either delivered to the home-based coder by the facility courier or the coder may have to come into the hospital or facility to pick them up.

Communicating with the facility is extremely important. For the home-based coder, this can be facilitated through e-mail. On a daily basis, the facility can send any messages regarding the previous day's discharges and other information the coder may require for daily coding assignments.

Coders can be connected to the facility's computer system, engaging the system by entering his or her individual password. A manual coding book can be used for the coding; then abstracting is performed via modem to the hospital's abstracting system, entering diagnoses, procedures and codes into the computer. With the coding completed, the computer automatically notifies the billing department that the chart is ready for billing.

Some hospitals have begun utilizing home-based coding specialists, to enable the facilities to more easily recruit and retain coders. Often, qualified coders who live far from medical facilities are unwilling to travel the long distances required to perform in-house coding duties. By remaining home-based, the coders are happier and less stressed; and the health care facilities get their coding completed with excellent results and retain skilled coders for future work.

In the near future home-based coding opportunities will be expanding. As more medical record information becomes available online, home-based coding will be a reality for greater numbers of independent coders. This area opens up wonderful business opportunities. Although the CPR (computerized patient record) is on the increase, most hospitals are still paper-based, which means that copies of records need to be available for coders to review. Hospitals that do have documents available via computer technology can benefit from home-basing their coding specialists by interfacing them with their hospital data base through Internet technology.

Confidentiality is still a major issue where home-based coders are concerned. There are those who feel that since home-based medical transcriptionists have been successfully working with records for years, coders should be able to make a similar transition. However, others argue that unlike the medical transcriptionist who has only sections of the medical record, the coder works with the entire patient record, which presents greater potential for a breach of confidentiality. Whether or not home-based coding is riskier than home-based transcription will probably not be determined soon. However, because issues of confidentiality are of such concern, most hospitals and other health care facilities are hesitant to agree to home-based coding at the present time.

So, although home-based coding is not yet the norm, hospitals are definitely looking at this as a possible viable option for the future. They would benefit in a number of ways. Home-based coding would allow hospitals to outsource the cost center (some hospitals have outsourced their entire health information department, including the coding), increase in-house space availability, increase numbers of available qualified coders, downsize facility, contract instead of maintaining employees, etc.

Professionals in the industry agree that as increasing numbers of electronic patient record systems are implemented in more hospitals, home-based coding will begin to grow. When will this happen? We believe SOON.

THE MULTITALENTED CODER — EXPANDING YOUR HORIZONS

Training in Physician Offices

Physician office coding is a resource for contract coding. As health information professionals, coders can assist physicians as they begin their quest with RBRVS (resource-based relative value system). Interaction with the physician office setting is important and appropriate. Coders have the expertise to assist physicians and their staff in the area of coding and classification.

Coder training in the physician office setting is also a resourceful consulting service. The background and experience of physician office personnel has historically been medical office tasks, nurse, medical assistant, or clerk. Coding is a new frontier for them and they often lack the expertise and skills to adequately perform the job. Thus, the coding varies greatly from office to office, and how much time is devoted to coding accuracy and quality is undetermined. It is certain that inappropriate coding can result in poor reimbursement.

Coding and reimbursement go hand-in-hand in the physician office setting. The entire focus of coding in the physician office environment is to receive payment for services provided by the physician. This is somewhat different from the acute hospital setting where coding is performed for data collection purposes as stated elsewhere in this book (allowing for retrieval for research, quality assurance, etc.), in addition to reimbursement. However, physician office personnel have a difficult time accessing coding guidelines. The CPT is of greater importance in the physician office setting than ICD, because of CPT's direct link to reimbursement. The newsletter publication titled **CPT Assistant** is a new resource (see in resource section of this book) that is designed to assist with the interpretation of CPT codes and lead to guidelines for CPT coding. It gives practical tips for more accurate and efficient physician coding.

The coder in a physician's office generally codes what she is told will bring in payment, not necessarily the *appropriate* code. Physician office coders code what works, even though payers have their own rules and interpretation of various codes within their systems. Medicare says one thing, Blue Cross another, workers' compensation yet another. One must first know the payor to determine which guideline to use for coding diagnostic and procedural information.

Enter the superbill! A superbill is a checklist of ICD diagnostic codes and CPT procedure codes, commonly encountered/performed by the physician. This type billing method has been helpful for physician office coding because the coder does need to accurately link the diagnostic code with the appropriate procedure code. Physicians and/ or nurses are generally the ones responsible for checking the appropriate codes on the superbill, but they rarely perform the matching function. This is usually left to a less qualified physician office staff person who often lacks a clinical background.

Many physicians have converted from manual to automated billing systems or are considering doing so, and many of the new physician office software packages include a "coding package," which, although helpful, is generally very primitive and has limited ability to match the diagnosis with the proper service. Most of these software packages have been created by the payers, with very little input from providers as to their needs.

As a contract coder/consultant, you can be of great value and offer a very needed service to physicians and their personnel in the form of primary education supporting optimum reimbursement, general knowledge about coding and classification, as well as providing coding assistance. This may include assistance with ICD-9 and CPT coding requirements and information regarding upcoming educational programs and coding clinics that office staff may attend.

Assisting in the selection of software and providing software education is another area of expertise you can share with the physician and office staff, as well as evaluating the accuracy of superbills to make certain codes are used appropriately.

HOW CODING AND BILLING ARE LINKED IN THE OUTPATIENT SETTING

The diagnosis codes tell *why* the doctor performed the procedure; the CPT codes tell *what* he did. The link between diagnosis and CPT is becoming more and more important because of treatment protocols being instituted by insurance companies, utilization review for HMO, and managed care groups.

Consider the case of patient John Doe, whose insurance company refused to pay his medical bills, ruling his treatment was not indicated for his diagnosis. Why? Because Mr. Doe's recorded diagnosis was "abdominal pain", but John Doe had an arthroscopic knee procedure. Coding specialists must make certain that each condition the patient is being seen for is actually being coded. In John Doe's case, abdominal pain has no diagnostic link with a scope of the knee.

LEARNING OUTPATIENT CODING AND BILLING

Currently, there are few outpatient coding courses available. There are coding seminars that review what CPT codes are, how to code ICD-9 codes. And there are some coding classes at the community college level that are very general, providing an overview of what is done during outpatient billing/coding. However, all this is changing. There is a growing need for more experienced coding specialists entering the outpatient area. Many employees in outpatient billing departments have little or no knowledge of anatomy/physiology or other medical terminology, have not been educated in health care billing or coding, and much of their work is trial and error.

Experienced inpatient coding specialists have the opportunity to expand into and offer services in the outpatient area. If you are interested in moving in this direction and if you are an experienced inpatient coder who is skilled at evaluating and coding from medical records, chances are good you can be readily trained to do outpatient coding. You will need to learn about outpatient care in the clinical setting and understand the differences between inpatient and outpatient coding. For instance, DRGs are not used in outpatient coding, and the outpatient setting requires a number of types of coding books. Patients are seen more frequently in an outpatient setting than in the acute care facility, so a much broader range of codes is required, and required more frequently. As an outpatient coder, you will have to be very precise.

Outpatient coders have learned to code from what the doctor writes down. An experienced coder will take not only what the doctor says (because he may forget to document the EKG, stool guaiac and other laboratory procedures), but as in the inpatient setting, the outpatient coding specialist will review the record to be able to code accurately and completely.

Often, outpatient coding services are integrated with billing services. The superbill is still used widely, but not just for billing purposes. Now it is used more often for data entry, as a charge ticket. In the managed care setting, superbills are not used because with a flat fee for service, the patient is never billed. They may have to make a copayment at the time of service, but the physician office accepts whatever fee the health care provider (insurance company) will pay. These fees are generally negotiated through service contracts.

In the fee-for-service area where physicians can elect to participate or not participate, superbills are given directly to patients. In this situation patients pay for services in full (the total amount of their bills) and submit the superbills to their insurance carriers.

COMPUTER SETUP FOR OUTPATIENT CODING

Outpatient coders and billers are able to homebase. This requires a computer terminal which is interfaced with the billing/client service. The computer terminals can be linked directly with the client to pull off records necessary for coding/billing through a communication software such as PcAnywhere, CarbonCopy, ProComm Plus, etc. Stand-alone billing software is generally utilized or, if working for a physician office, the ability to dial into (interface with) the physician office and use their software. Some coding/billing services also offer medical transcription services.

REFERENCE MATERIALS FOR OUTPATIENT CODING

The CPT and ICD-9 code books will be two of your primary references: ICD-9 for diagnosis, CPT for procedure codes. As described elsewhere, the CPT codes are the common procedure terminology codes used by all outpatient and private practices. These references must be updated yearly. Other outpatient coding references include the McGraw-Hill RVS coding books, CRVS coding books, California official Medical Fee Schedule for Workers' Compensation, Nevada official Workers' Compensation Fee schedule. RBRVS codes, Medicare Fee Schedules. Other references include anatomy books, specialty code books for dermatology, plastic and reconstructive surgery, physical therapy, orthopedics, etc., CPT-assistant for Definition (published by the AMA).

In addition, individual physician contracts refer to the fee schedule being used for each contract and how the individual physician contract applies to that fee schedule.

In summary, a broad knowledge base is necessary in the outpatient coding arena the same as in the inpatient coding arena. If you are good at what you do, the business will come. Frequently, coding specialists have very little need for marketing their services because their businesses have successfully evolved through word-of-mouth referrals. That is, your clients recommend your service to others.

ALTERNATIVE CAREERS FOR THE CODING SPECIALIST

"Great opportunities are always around. Successful people watch for and take advantage of them."

If you are already an experienced coder, you may want to explore alternative career paths that will be available because of your background and knowledge. A few of these alternatives are discussed on the following pages of this text.

TUMOR REGISTRY

In bygone days cancer information was recorded by hand, about patients in hospitals. This was done by clerks and secretaries. As the cancer programs continue to grow and mature, the recording of this information has evolved to include computer data entry.

The role of the tumor registry is to gather information about the incidence of cancer in designated populations. This is an indispensable tool in tracking and trending the disease. With access to reliable statistics on the occurrence of different types of cancer, the people affected, treatment provided and other epidemiological factors, researchers and public health officials are better able to identify problems and evaluate remedies. Findings from these studies include environmental influences on the development of neoplasms, susceptibility of certain ethnic and social groups to particular neoplasms, and the need for oncology services in various locales, information for health professionals and citizens regarding specific health risks, early detection and treatment, and appropriateness of diagnostic and therapeutic procedures.

The tumor registry maintains a register of cancer patients and pertinent data about their condition. Many hospitals have their own cancer registries. The purpose of a hospital registry is to provide physicians with data needed to maintain quality of care through peer review and to compare performance with recognized standards.

A hospital must report every case of inpatient and outpatient cancer first seen there. Information from tumor registries is gathered for use in research and for monitoring the occurrence of cancer in various regions. As a result of the registry, valuable statistics have been developed about the treatment and survival of cancer patients.

Information about cancer cases is reported in the form of abstracts which summarize pertinent information about individual cases. Although some areas still report by hand, in many regions specialized computer software is available for preparing abstracts in accordance with reporting requirements. Whichever system is used, rules for entering data must be followed precisely. Much of the information is entered in codes consisting of numbers and characters. There are certain reference works for coding (International Classification of Diseases for Oncology, Geneva: WHO).

The principal sources for identifying cancer patients are found in the patient record and in the disease indexes (codes assigned by coders). If you have a solid professional background in coding, working in a tumor registry is a viable option to incorporate into your independent business.

EDUCATION AND TRAINING FOR TUMOR REGISTRY WORK

Knowledge is the foundation for reliable data collection. Anatomy, physiology, and understanding of the cancer disease process are vital components of a registrar's education, not dissimilar to the requirements for coding specialists. The types of initial tumor registry training available are the following:

1) Certificate program . . . Two weeks to three months
   Junior college program . . . Two years (associate degree)
   College program . . . Four years (baccalaureate degree)

2) On-the-job instruction is always part of the initial training. Continuing education is essential to reinforce the foundation of basic knowledge and to train registrars in current techniques for cancer diagnostic staging, treatment, data analysis and research. Additional registry-related training is available from a variety of sources, including local, state and national registry professional associations, adult education courses in the health sciences, and a growing library of reference materials.

For more information on working in a tumor registry contact:

Commission on Cancer
55 East Erie Street
Chicago, Illinois 60611
312-664-4050

National Tumor Registrars Association
505 E. Hawley Street
Mundelein, IL 60060
708-566-0833

Tumor Registry and Support
H.I.M. Solutions, Inc.
800-289-8854 Florida, New York, New Jersey

MEDICAL RECORD ABSTRACTING FOR SEVERITY OF ILLNESS

Many hospitals are developing abstracting computer systems to analyze patient medical records for determining the "severity of illness" for that hospital's inpatient encounter. Hospital coders are being trained in analyzing the chart and retrieving and imputing this information into a computer system. Hospitals then use the coded data to educate staff in ways of providing quality care improvement. Check local hospitals for possible contract needs.

THE RECOVERY SPECIALIST

Most billing services do not provide recovery services. This is a service in which specialists audit medical practices. For example, when a physician practice has had an incidence of embezzlement from an employee or where the billing has been put in a drawer for six months, never mailed or never done, a recovery specialist will audit every chart in the practice and identify things that were not billed or were underbilled. The recovery specialist will then rebill, submit appeals for greater reimbursement, etc. In some cases recovery revenues are in the thousands of dollars. Delayed billing alone can result in substantial reduced reimbursement, so recovery specialists can provide a very significant, cost-effective, revenue-producing service to their clients. By improving the client's cash flow, the recovery specialist can be a hero to the client.

FEES FOR THE RECOVERY SPECIALIST

Generally the recovery specialist bases his or her fees on the amount of revenues collected, e.g., twenty-five percent of revenue recovered, etc. This is negotiated on a client-by-client basis, taking into account the task(s) at hand involved in the recovery process.

SETTING UP BUSINESS OPERATIONS

*"Time spent organizing your business is one of
your best investments."*

Streamlined organization results in working smarter, not harder. As your business grows and your day-to-day operations become more complex, you will almost certainly be faced with the daunting task of how to get everything done in a normal workday. The answer is to work smarter not harder. Think ahead and plan the use of your resources. Use the know-how and skills you have acquired to accomplish the multiple demands made on your time.

PLANNING AND IMPLEMENTING

Your plan should include deciding what, how and when the various tasks will be done.

- Set objectives and include ways to cut costs and raise productivity.

- Establish clear-cut standards of practice.

- Actively seek out ideas of peers before deciding on a course of action.

- Organize a plan for tackling large projects.

- Match skills to tasks when making assignments.

- Monitor your performance and assess available resources.

- Pride yourself on a job well done.

Remember, if you have a good plan of action you are on the road to working smarter, not harder. If you don't seem to be moving forward, you may be trying to do too much yourself. Slow down, set goals, develop an action plan, and delegate whenever feasible.

THE OFFICE ENVIRONMENT

Whether you plan to perform on-site coding or home-based coding, you still need a homebase for your business. A well-designed, organized work environment is essential to the smooth operation of a coding business. Some of these benefits include the following:

- Smoother, more efficient flow of paperwork

- Maximum use of automation

- Simplified operating procedures that require minimum movement of staff and equipment

- Fewer work stoppages and delays

- Room for expansion

- Better working conditions

- Comfort and satisfaction

The office layout and decor should be both workable and pleasing. A well planned and attractive office will make you feel good and inspire you to work harder. An unattractive, poorly designed office may depress you and cause your productivity to decline.

Considerations for office planning:

- Overall needs for your coding business

- Physical facilities available

- Location

- Special functions required
    Work
    Privacy
    Storage
    Files and supplies

- Computer equipment requirements

- Office equipment and other furnishings

Make sure you will be working uninterrupted in a quiet environment, have privacy for conducting telephone calls, and adequate security to protect confidentiality of the database you will be working with.

Other factors to consider will include sound, layout, lighting, and office furnishings.

BEING THE BOSS MEANS FLEXIBLE HOURS

You are the boss, so you can enjoy flexibility in scheduling your working hours to accommodate your family and career. You will find that most clients are willing to be flexible, too, and adapt to your schedule.

Being the boss also means that you can pick and choose your clients. You may choose clients within a specific mileage range from your home. If you are booked solid or if you wish to take a break from your office, you can turn away work or refer it to other contract services. There is great satisfaction in knowing that you can work as little or as much as you want.

EQUIPMENT NEEDS

Your personal equipment needs will vary depending on your work situation. If you are a coding employee, the facility you work for may provide the computer equipment you must have. On the other hand, if you work as an independent home-based coder, you will be required to provide your own equipment.

ERGONOMICS

When setting up your office, don't neglect ergonomic (the study of movement) factors. A physically well-designed work setting that allows your body to work as efficiently and as easily as possible is the goal of work place ergonomics, and you should make sure your working environment is a healthy one. Before buying, get advice on keyboards, trays, monitor placement, chairs, forearm supports, furniture, work surface accessories, lighting and glare, and posture.

There are a variety of keyboards on the market with various features that promote good posture and good positioning. Because everyone's body habitus is different, what is ergonomically correct for one may be incorrect for another.

For more information on ergonomic systems, contact KARE Products. This company offers a product catalog and an ergonomic guide that has been approved by ergonomists and health providers.

KARE Products
ERGOCARE, Inc.
www.careproducts.com

REFERENCE BOOKS AND OTHER RESOURCES

There a many coding reference books and other resources that will facilitate your coding/consulting work, keep you up to date on current coding guidelines and help you stay on top of the latest industry trends. For a complete list of our favorites, see "Favorite References and Resources" at the back of this book.

FORMS

To do your coding job you will need to organize the appropriate materials to perform your services efficiently. Two important forms are the DRG work sheet and the DRG billing form. (See examples in appendix).

The work sheet is completed for each chart reviewed. You can provide information on the original codes, recommended changes, and comments. The work sheet is reviewed with the department manager who agrees or disagrees with the recommendations, and signs off on the form.

The billing form is basically a log of your charges. This is submitted to the client with your invoice for reference.

LICENSING AND REGULATIONS

Studies show that among self-employed individuals, 95% of those who succeed in business have obtained business licenses. Entrepreneurial consultants are not surprised by this pattern. They believe that obtaining a business license is a primary indicator of the commitment and planning necessary for career success.

In many states, you will probably be required by town, county, or state to have a business license. However, some rural areas are excluded from this requirement. Required or not, a business license may be helpful to you. Many banks will not open a business account without verification of licensing and, in addition, operating a business without a required license can result in fines and business closure.

The first step in acquiring your business license is to investigate your city and county codes and zoning restrictions. If you are in a residential neighborhood there may be stricter policies than in commercial zones. Check on rules and regulations at the zoning department at your city hall or county administration office. If you live in a small town, you may only need to go to the city hall, fill out a request to operate a home-based personal service and obtain a business license. Usually, your business license must be renewed each year.

On the application, you will probably be asked whether or not your business operation will create additional pedestrian/auto traffic. If yours is a personal service in which you provide pick up and delivery with no clients coming in and out, your business should easily meet legal requirements. On the other hand, if your business will increase traffic, you may face restrictions. Standards vary so check with your city, county, or state on local zoning regulations before opening your doors to business.

When processing your business license, double check your assigned business classification and the fee rate. Most city clerks do not understand the work of a medical coder so they may classify you incorrectly and charge you an excessive license fee. We have found that business license fees generally average $50 to $75. If you are charged over that amount, don't hesitate to question the licensing clerk.

ESTABLISHING FEES FOR SERVICES

"You need to know how to code baby heart surgery."

Susan Brown, ART

As with any business, you must determine what your rates for varying services will be. If your rates are set too high, you will price yourself out of the market; if too low, you won't receive the compensation your expertise deserves and you will also do a disservice to your fellow coders by undercutting their prices and devaluing their skills.

It is impossible within the confines of this book to give specific rates as the variables are too great. What part of the country will you be working in? In what type of facility? How much competition will you have and what are their rates? Hourly rates may range from a low of $20 to $50 and up; per-chart rates, from $10 for Medicare coding to $65 and up.

MARKET RESEARCH

In order to establish appropriate fees for services rendered, you will need to do some market research. Preliminary investigation can begin quite easily, simply by networking with your peers at local meetings and online services. Your fees should be based on the number of years of coding experience doing inpatient versus outpatient coding. Medicare (DRG) experience is a major factor in salary ranges.

> "If you are going to work independently, you must expect to be exposed to a variety of coding environments. If you are providing coding services to acute care hospitals be prepared to code what you are told to code, and expect to meet hospital productivity standards if applicable. You will need to have a very wide range of experience in all types of acute care coding. You may be asked to code procedures in which you have had no experience at all in coding."
>
> If you find yourself in a skill area that is beyond your level of expertise, be honest with your clients and ask for help. You can also refer to your resources for help with coding difficult cases. Your clients will respect your honesty and you will preserve your credibility. Consider this type of situation a learning experience that you can carry with you to your next assignment."
>
> -Susan Brown, ART

You'll learn much by networking with other coding consultants and managers who utilize the services of consultants. If all else fails, sign on with a reputable coding service. You can expect to be offered some contracts on an hourly basis; some on a per-chart basis. You can then add a minimum of thirty percent over what you receive from the service to determine what you will charge your own clients. Remember, though, that you can negotiate rates on a per-assignment basis even with coding services.

A word of caution: You will probably be asked to sign a contract which prohibits you from obtaining your own contract with the services' clients for a period of one year after severing your contract with the service. Maintain ethical practices at all times both with your own clients and with a coding service. Remember, negative word-of-mouth travels fast in this field.

RATE VARIABLES

The rates you charge for your coding services will vary depending on your years of experience and the different insurance types, e.g., Medicare versus non-Medicare records, inpatient records, outpatient surgery or other outpatient x-ray/laboratory services, emergency room records, etc. Medicare (DRG experience) will be a major factor in setting your fees. Keep in mind, you will be expected to meet hospital productivity standards. If you are coding less than in-house coders but charging the client more, you may not last long. Productivity is important.

What you charge on a per-chart basis will vary depending on chart types. For instance, for inpatient coding, the fee charged may be increased for coding Medicare charts. DRG optimization background is essential for this type of coding. If your contract includes both types of inpatient coding, stipulate the increase in fees for DRG coding. Also be sure to include an additional fee if abstracting is involved.

OUTPATIENT SURGERY CODING

Outpatient surgery coding may require the use of ICD-9-CM and CPT coding. Most if not all facilities will require both on all insurance types. Reimbursement is usually based on the CPT codes in this coding area. Knowledge of CPT is very important for the correct payment. Your fee charged should remain the same for all insurance types for outpatient surgery coding.

EMERGENCY ROOM, LABORATORY/X-RAY CODING

Check options at local hospitals for coding emergency room, laboratory/x-ray records. This area of coding may be the perfect opportunity for you to set up a system in your home. Many hospitals already contract with independents for this coding. The information needed to code these records can be copied, faxed or couriered to the home-based coder, coded and returned to the facility via courier. The home-based coder can also be technically networked with the facility computerized patient record and download records for coding purpose. Coding can then be accomplished online, and the record forwarded to the billing department through the integrated computer system.

Consider offering very reasonable rates for in-home coding services. Fees can be based on a weekly, or monthly basis for number of charts coded. For example: The department has an average of 150 records per week. You agree to a flat fee of $XXXX per week up to 175 charts. If the number of charts coded exceeds 175 in any given week, an additional fee is assessed per chart coded over 175. This allows a "window" for the client but also protects you from being inundated with an excess of records to code beyond the estimate of 150 charts quoted by the client.

MARKETING YOUR CODING SERVICES

"If you really want to succeed, you must learn how to market your services."

Marketing your business effectively is essential if your business is to succeed. Take time to learn what marketing is, establish a marketing plan that suits your business and personality, and move forward with determination and consistency. Soon, if your marketing is successful, your efforts will be rewarded as your business prospers and you enjoy professional success.

COLLECTING THE FACTS

Collecting the facts about the total market demand, competition, industry trends and other significant issues related to your target market will enable you to familiarize yourself with the resources in your area. If you are already established in the area you are targeting, you may already be aware of much of this information. On the other hand, if you are new to an area, there are various resources for obtaining market information.

Evaluate the overall need of the medical community in your area and then target a specific segment of that need. This will be your target market.

EVALUATING YOUR BACKGROUND AND EXPERIENCE

Evaluating your background and experience will help determine your target market. The more experience you have, the more diversified your service can become. Are you currently employed as a coder in an acute-care setting, clinic or outpatient setting? Each of these will have a different target market. If you are new to the field of coding, your target market will probably be limited. As you develop a higher level of skill and more confidence, consider expanding your business.

WARNING: Don't take on too much too soon!

If this is your first venture into independence, take it slow. Allow yourself time to become familiar with the disciplines required to maintain independence, develop additional skills if necessary, insights into your work style and build self-confidence.

You will probably have many choices. You may prefer to work as an independent contractor on-site, subcontract for a coding agency/service, or work home-based.

> *"For many independent coders, working for a coding contract service that utilizes independent contract coders is an excellent choice while establishing your business."*

EVALUATING YOUR MARKET AND COMPETITION

As you are researching the service demand in your area you will get a sense of whether there is a demand for coding services or whether the market is saturated. Contact local health care facilities to inquire about coding opportunities. Make phone inquiries and check out the trends in your area. Analyzing and investigating this data will help you determine the potential market for your coding services.

WHAT IS NEEDED

Think about what services you will be providing your clients. For acute care facilities and coding inpatient charts you will be required to use ICD-9-CM and CPT-4 coding systems as appropriate. Your services may include coding, optimizing, attestation preparation and transmittal, including messages to physicians, preparation of face sheet and coding summary, preparation and transmittal of additional coding summaries for requesting physicians, data entry, and other tasks necessary to complete the coding processing at a particular facility. Although attestations are no longer required by regulating bodies, many facilities still utilize them as a cover sheet on the chart, for physicians to view the diagnoses and procedures that were done (coded), along with a summary for billing services.

Health care facilities will provide access to necessary equipment and forms for record processing; however, you the coder may provide your own references for coding.

Coding roundtables are available in every state/region. Locate one in your area and make efforts to attend these regularly. You will benefit from a variety of discussions about the health care market. Roundtables are also a good place to introduce yourself and meet potential clients.

Networking with other coders will give you and your business additional exposure. Be sure to pass out your business card. Never hesitate to promote your business as word-of-mouth referrals may be readily passed on.

Review the weekly medical record magazines such as *Advance* and *For the Record*, where position want ads are published. Donate door prizes in your business name at appropriate professional functions. Advertise in trade publications, through association newsletters, and other professional sources.

FLIERS

A flier is one of the easiest and least expensive advertising methods. It should be clever, to capture the attention of the reader, but not too "cute." Avoid flowers and critters that tend to create a less than professional image of you and your business.

Create your own flier, or use the services of a local desktop publishing firm to help you design a professional piece. It will be a worthwhile expenditure of approximately $35-$50. Fliers can be in the form of a well-designed business brochure that conveys the message that you and your coding business are professional and successful. This will attract clients.

Your business flier should briefly identify your services and state your objectives. Do not quote a price in your flier. Details about your background experience and pricing should be presented only during discussions and negotiations with clients. Be sure to staple a business card to your flier when you mail it out. This will increase the odds that either the business card or the flier will be kept by the client for future reference.

When mailing out a flier, be sure to send it to the "chief financial officer" (CFO) or "administrator of finance" in the hospital, as well as the medical record director or health information manager. The bottom line is this: hospitals don't get paid if the accounts have not been coded appropriately for billing. You can help them get paid more and/or quicker by providing effective (accurate) coding services.

GETTING YOUR FIRST CLIENT

> *"Pay attention to the impression you make and people will pay attention to you."*

Getting out there to market yourself doesn't come easy for most of us. Marketing is perhaps the most difficult part of building a business, but it is also ninety percent of the success of a business. Many businesses can become well established through word-of-mouth referrals, but getting that first client can be the most difficult step forward in building your business, and a key to success will be the creation of value in the eyes of your clients.

Before you begin thinking about getting out in the big, wide world to market yourself, get organized. Think the process through from beginning to end.

PROSPECTIVE CLIENTS

- Hospitals
- Outpatient Centers
- Outpatient Surgery
- Same Day Care

- Skilled Nursing Facilities
- Rehabilitation Centers
- Psychiatric Hospitals/clinics
- Hospice
- Home Health
- Physician Offices
- Billing Services
- Insurance Companies
- Government Health Agencies
- Dentists
- Chiropractors
- Medical Labs

THE POWER RESUME

In order to market your services effectively, you will need to begin with a *power resume*. This should include your job target, your capabilities, accomplishments, work history, and your education and training.

Warm up by imagining yourself as the client. You want someone who you feel will provide more value than cost. You want someone with the right knowledge, training, skills and abilities, good character and one who will perform well. Someone who will provide a quality service that will help make your business or department a success. As you are developing your resume, keep the client's needs in perspective. Now begin building your resume. Keep in mind there is more than one type of resume. You may want to experiment with several different formats before you select one or two that will suit your needs. Here are some alternative approaches to resume formats:

Functional resume: Highlights your skills or areas of expertise. This is a particularly good approach if your job target requires specific, definable skills.

Chronological resume: Emphasizes your career path and experience. It describes the jobs held starting with the most recent. This is the most traditional way of submitting a resume.

Targeted resume: The targeted resume style emphasizes your capabilities, the ability to create future value, supported by past accomplishments. This resume format is attractive to many because it focuses on future opportunity.

THE POWER LETTER

Every resume you send should be accompanied by a personalized letter. This should be your *power letter*. Your personal introduction to your prospective clients, inviting them to review your resume. Here are a few tips about writing your power letter.

Write your letter to a real person — get a name and title, and make sure you verify the correct spelling. Most people feel insulted when they receive a letter with their name misspelled, and it doesn't make a good first impression. If you are unsure of the contact person's name, call the facility or department and ask for the department manager's or director's name, spelling of the name, departmental title and correct address. Before printing your letter, double check spelling on each item to be mailed.

Make sure you send your letter to a decision maker. Start the letter with an opening paragraph that will catch the attention of the reader. Focus your letter on what you can contribute. Emphasize your awareness of the department needs and turnaround. Clearly state what you have to offer and express yourself with "friendly" confidence. Close the letter with a request for action, such as an interview or follow-up phone call. "I would be happy to discuss my qualifications with you further."

Make your letter look terrific, but keep it to one page. This initial letter should be an example of the care that you put into your work. Be sure to check the letter for spelling, grammar and punctuation mistakes, print it on good bond paper, and mail in a quality envelope.

PROSPECTIVE CLIENT FOLLOW-UP

Be sure and follow up your letter with a phone call a week or two later. If you make it to the interview stage, be sure and follow up the interview with another letter or thank-you note.

Never close the door to future opportunities. Even if there is currently no need for your services, let potential clients know that you will check back with them periodically. Then, continue to follow up with periodic phone calls.

KEEP TRACK OF YOUR CONTACTS

It's a good idea to make a contact log of all clients to whom you have submitted resumes. This log should include the date sent, contact name, business name, phone number, fax number, status and comments. This is good business practice, and you will appreciate being able to refer to details in this log for future contacts.

CLIENT RELATIONSHIPS

Sometimes, a consultant-client relationship that is too close may become a problem. Intimate friendships, which usually include a sense of personal responsibility to make your friend happy, may confuse professional issues and responsibilities and make it more difficult to resolve problems. Keep in mind, there will come a time when you will have to renegotiate a contract with that person, and being a good-buddy friend will not make this easier. Your client may expect you to be more generous, beyond what is professionally practical, because you have a close personal relationship.

Our advice is to maintain a consistent professional relationship with clients, and keep your personal and social life separate.

THE INTERVIEW

Sitting for an interview is very stressful for most people, usually because they lack the professional skills and experience necessary to handle interviews confidently and successfully. Being well prepared at the time you present yourself for an interview is extremely important. Following are some key factors to consider as you are organizing yourself for the interview process. Successful interviews result from attention to details.

- Don't chew gum.

- Think about what services you are prepared to offer and, from the client's point of view, why you should be given the opportunity to provide those services.

- Learn about and fully understand the client's needs and how you can meet those needs.

- Anticipate questions and rehearse your response — answers and issues you wish to clarify and discuss.

- Practice being positive, alert and enthusiastic.

- Prepare an agenda for the interview listing the points you want to make. To be successful in the interview, you must subtly manage the direction of the interview process; do not merely follow the lead of the interviewer.

- Prior to the interview, stand in front of a mirror and practice aloud what you will say, evaluating and improving your posture, voice modulation and phrasing. During the interview, be aware of and stay alert to your word usage, innuendo and body language as well as that of the interviewer.

WHAT TO BRING WITH YOU TO THE INTERVIEW

Arrive at the interview with **all** materials you will need — note portfolio, resume, references, list of current clients, note paper, pen, and other items important to this meeting. Organize the various pieces of information so you know where they are and don't have to fumble searching for them. You'll be more confident if everything is in order.

THE WINNING IMAGE

Interviewers (clients) base their decision on tangible and intangible factors. *Tangible* factors include visual, physical, material images — dress, education, past experience and accomplishments. *Intangible* factors include those things that cannot be perceived by the senses — confidence, responsiveness, preparedness, energy and enthusiasm.

Following are tips we have found useful:

- Be on time. Be sure to map out directions ahead of time and arrive with time to spare. If the route seems at all confusing, call the client's office or other dependable source for specific information on freeways, exits and other details that will prevent delays.

- Before, during and after every interview, believe in and trust yourself, confident that you are the solution to a problem, and that your clients need you more than you need them.

- During the interview process find out how and by whom the final decision will be made.

- Be prepared to discuss some of your past successes that demonstrate your qualifications to perform services for this client.

- During the interview, remember to keep track of the time and, if necessary, refer to your notes (neatly organized and readily available in your portfolio).

> *"Sitting for an interview is very stressful for most people, usually because they lack the professional skills and experience necessary to handle interviews confidently and successfully."*

WHAT NOT TO DO

"How to change your stinkin' thinkin'"

—Kerry Hein

More often than not, what we do not do is as important as what we do. Consider the following:

- Avoid negativity, gossip, complaining and indirect comments. If have nothing positive to say ... don't say anything.

- Avoid tentative words such as "I hope," "I'll do my best," "I'll try," "more or less." Such phrases do not instill confidence in potential clients.

- Avoid talking too much. Answer each question positively but succinctly, avoiding long stories about yourself.

- Promote your business but don't **push** it. There is a fine line between confidently recommending your service while maintaining the client's dignity and an unappealing, arrogance-tinged sales pitch that demeans the interviewer's business.

Compare the following examples:

Threatening: "I think I can get your mess cleaned up pretty fast and get everything back into shape and current."

Nonthreatening: "I think I can help you bring the coding up to date."

- Never speak negatively about clients.

- Never express neediness.

CLOSING THE INTERVIEW

As you close the interview, recap the benefits that you offer. Make a proposition by offering to provide services on a provisional basis for a period of time. If all goes well, a contract can be negotiated. Plant a seed ... "I look forward to speaking with you again soon."

Send a letter to the prospective client within 48-hours of the interview, reiterating your key propositions and offering your services. Make this a one-page letter, relevant and interesting. You will be looked upon favorably if the letter also includes a thank you with the above.

If the interview goes badly, use the next couple of days to recap, rebuild your self-confidence and make more thorough preparation for the next interview.

Follow up with a phone call about a week after the interview. Make plans for long-term follow-up of client contacts. Keep a client log and document follow-up after a week, four weeks, six months, twelve months, etc.

To be successful you must know your value in the business world and communicate it over and over again until you make the right connections. Good luck!

NETWORKING AND ADVERTISING

One of the best resources for coding information is AHIMA (American Health Information Management Association), and we recommend that you join this organization. Membership entitles you to membership in most state/regional associations at no extra charge. As a member you will have the opportunity to network with your peers at professional meetings and conventions and seminars, have access to journals, newsletters and other publications that provide valuable references for coders and other health care professionals.

"NET"WORKING

Become familiar with online services and the Internet if you are not already. The Internet is a great resource for networking. There are many health care Web sites, organization Web sites, and an excellent resource to weave through these is *NetPractice, A Beginner's Guide to Healthcare Networking on the Internet*, by Mary Frances Miller. This book is written by a health care professional, not a computer professional. It is a self-instructional, practical guide that assumes you know nothing about the Internet, and is very easy to follow.

Contact Opus Communications at 617-639-1872/Fax 617-639-2982, or e-mail: customer_service@opuscomm.com. Visit their Web site http://www.opuscomm.com.

We have referred to several Web sites elsewhere in this book, however, web pages are like paid advertisements and can come and go with time. It is impossible to guarantee that the resources that are referred to at the time of this writing will still be available online in the future.

MAINTAINING A PROFESSIONAL IMAGE AND ATTITUDE — TEN TIPS TO INSPIRE CONFIDENCE

Presenting yourself as a credible professional is essential to your success as an independent coder. To convey this image you must dress appropriately and act professionally at all times, even if you're having a bad hair day.

- Act confidently, always.
- Dress the part.
- Be tidy, clean and well groomed.
- Look your clients in the eye.
- Have your facts available.
- Do your homework.
- When you don't know something, admit it! Then, as soon as possible, find the information you were lacking and update your client.
- Carry a well-organized briefcase.
- Always smile.
- Be five minutes early for all appointments.

CODING CONTRACTS

*Contract: An agreement between two or more parties,
especially one written and enforceable by law.*

Now that you have made the decision to pursue your career as an independent health care coder, you will need to develop a contract that will suit your needs and those of your clients. Following are guidelines we have found helpful during our careers as independent coding specialists:

- **Identify yourself/service:** Your business letterhead will be appropriate.

- **Identify the parties in the agreement:** Include your name/ business name and facility name.

- **Set forth your objective:** Clarify what you are trying to accomplish for the client (e.g., assure accurate coding of the medical record).

- **Scope of service:** Specify how you will accomplish the objective. Itemize or briefly state what services you will provide.

- **Compensation:** Include your fee schedule, with updates as necessary, how often and in what manner you will submit your statements/bills for services. Include specific information about when payment is due, suspension of services for nonpayment, and reinstatement of service following payment.

- **Relationship between Consultant and Health Care Facility:** Clearly state that the relationship between you and the facility is that of an independent contractor and not that of employer/employee.

- **Confidentiality of Records:** Clearly state your position regarding confidentiality of all medical information obtained in the facility and from its records.

- **Term of the Agreement:** Include the date the agreement begins, how long it will remain in effect, the conditions of termination by either party, procedures for notification, and time limits.

- **Signatures:** Include your or your representative's signature and the signature of the facility representative. Send the original to facility and keep a copy for your records.

"Beware handshake agreements. The hand that shook yours so eagerly in the beginning may later slap you in the face."
— Caleb Cornell

VERBAL CONTRACTS

Occasionally you may enter into an agreement with a client who does not wish to sign a written contract. In this case, make sure that you keep accurate records, copies of invoices, and copies of payment checks you have received from the facility. This will provide added assurance (proof) that a verbal agreement (word-of-mouth) did exist.

CONTRACT DECISIONS — THE DETAILS!

Developing your contract will depend on a wide variety of issues:

- Hourly fee vs. per chart fee; basic lump sum fee per contract; needs such as continuing education workshops or quality assessment.

- Where you perform the contract — at the facility vs. in-home coding.

- Type of charts being coded: inpatient/outpatient surgery/ER/ OP, physician office charts, etc. (which will entail ICD-9-CM and/or CPT).

- Types of insurance: Medicare (which has DRG needs) vs. non-Medicare.

- Abstracting issues

- Computer response time as well as data entry needs. (Believe me, they vary greatly!)

123

● Audits per chart required with each facility.

● Organization of the medical records department/physician offices/or the type of facility you are considering.

● Availability of encoder system.

CONTRACT DECISIONS — OTHER INFORMATION

In order to make wise contract decisions, carefully evaluate each of the following issues.

● **Coding guidelines per facility**. Basic AHIMA coding guidelines should be the foundation, plus added guidelines for each facility's own needs.

● **Productivity standards.** Learn about the productivity standards and performance requirements of the in-house coders.

● **Basic day-to-day needs**. You wouldn't want to arrive and find out that there are only three charts for you to code that day. During the contracting process, make it clear what your time and chart needs for each day's work will be. Request to see the case-mix index for the previous six months. If your contract includes inpatient Medicare coding, ask for a longer term contract, and at least one full month for coding Medicare. Asking for the above items will be most helpful if you have solid experience with DRGs. Increase in case-mix index is always a plus for your continued coding support (acute care hospital).

●**Unbilled List.** Knowing something about the facility's "unbilled list" may also prove useful. The unbilled list is a report indicating the total dollar amount the facility has not billed due to uncoded charts. It is separated by inpatient discharges or outpatient discharges, showing each patient's discharge with total charges for that account/admission. A/R (accounts receivable) days are very important to most hospitals. If the charts have not been coded, facilities usually cannot bill the account. And that means that potential incoming cash is unduly deferred.

THE DIRECTOR'S CONCERNS

Quality, Quality, Quality. Some directors are concerned that a per-chart fee might compromise the quality of the coding and may need some reassurance if you are considering this payment option. Will you be as "thorough" if your payments are based on how many charts you code? If so, and if you are very fast and know that your coding quality is above average, then by all means consider a per-chart fee. You may significantly increase your revenue via a per-chart fee arrangement.

CONTRACT MANAGEMENT

In the current health care environment of managed care and capitation, institutions are turning to contract management in increasing numbers. This segment of the contract management market is expected to grow substantially in upcoming years as hospitals look beyond simple cost reduction to providing optimal value throughout the institution.

A fairly new area of contract management is contract health information management, which offers a variety of financial and efficiency benefits. Some of the red flags that may indicate the need for coding contract services may include the following:

- Unbilled accounts exceeding six days of revenue

- Frequent personnel turnover

- Case-mix index not where it should be

- Prospective payments not optimized

- Excessive numbers of delinquent records

In bidding for contracts you must be competitive in the marketplace. When you are considering submitting a bid for a contract, evaluate the qualities that you have to offer to fulfill the job:

Adequate experience and expertise to do the job. You must be able to convince clients that you can do the job and that they will be gaining something by contracting with you (an increase in hospital reimbursement, and reduction in operating costs, or both).

Mutually agreeable objectives and performance criteria (unbilled account levels, coding quality, turnaround time, etc.).

Shared risk. You must assume the risk of your day-to-day operations.

Guaranteed performance. You should guarantee present performance goals at an agreed upon price.

Quality. You should maintain ongoing, aggressive training and professional development skills.

Awareness. It is your responsibility to provide quality service and stay informed about regulatory and health care management trends and changes that affect coding.

ENCODER SOFTWARE

*"Hurrah for those who develop the software
that meets the needs of America's new industries!"*

With the advent of the Prospective Payment System, encoder software systems have become as common as color-coded filing systems in health information (medical records) departments. Promises of increased reimbursement and coder productivity have sold these systems to hospitals' chief financial officers. However, optimized reimbursement and increased coder productivity are not the only criteria necessary to evaluate a tool which builds the hospital's most valuable information asset, the clinical data base.

Computer hardware vendors often compare their products with various benchmark tests for speed. Medical records directors, as the clinical information managers, also need benchmarks to measure the value of an encoder for the selection of complete, accurate and consistent codes that not only optimize reimbursement but also support analysis and management of the hospital product — quality patient care. The health information manager also needs to consider the effect this technology has on the development and enhancement of coder skills.

HOW DOES THE ENCODER "THINK"?

How does the encoder "think"? This software is a knowledge-based system; a tool to assist, not just automate complex decision-making processes. Unlike a relational data base that organizes facts in predefined categories, these systems duplicate the structure and logic of a body of knowledge.

An encoder is the in-house consultant who knows the references and has the right answer to whatever coding question occurs. An encoder enhances but is not a substitute for the knowledge of a "human" coder.

ENCODER PROS AND CONS

A number of companies have developed coding software. This software is generally known as an encoder. While the availability of enhancements has improved immensely over the past few years, i.e., Coding clinic online, CPT Crosswalk, Medical Dictionary and Body Works™ accessible in a windows environment, the coding logic, that is the process used to arrive at a correct code, is basically of two types: **Expert** or **book logic** and **tree logic**. Finding a code using the book logic encoder is just what the name implies — the coder enters main terms, sub-terms and so on in a similar manner to using an ICD-9 code book. The tree logic encoder, however, requires the entry of only the main term, at which point the encoder presents a series of questions whose answers lead to a code selection.

There are pros and cons for both logics, and there are probably as many opinions about which one is best as there are coders. However, we have yet to meet a coder who, after using any encoder, would vote for going back to simply using a book! If nothing else, an encoder frees us from the tedium of paging through a book.

As a contractor/consultant, it is to your advantage to have a working knowledge of as many encoders as possible. You may be asked to code using the facility's encoder or asked for your opinions at facilities considering the initial purchase of an encoder or a change to a different encoder.

You may also find yourself acting as an unofficial trainer, helping in-house staff through the learning process during encoder installations. Expert knowledge of encoders can also provide business opportunities with software companies as they utilize experienced coders to help them with development, improvement, and installation training of their product.

Keep in mind, however, that you may work in facilities that do not use encoders, or they may not have a computer station available for your use, so keep an updated code book handy and maintain the skills necessary to use it efficiently.

If you are interested in learning more in-depth information about what encoder software has to offer, here are a few resources:

3M
P.O. Box 57900
575 West Murray Blvd.
Murray, Utah 84157

Medicus
One Rotary Center, Suite 1111
Evanston, Illinois 60201

Codemaster Corporation
10 South Riverside Plaza, Suite 1510
Chicago, Illinois 60606

Cascade
IRP Systems, Inc.
One Presidential Way, Suite 109
Woburn, MA 01801

BUILDING A SUCCESSFUL CODING/CONSULTING BUSINESS

"The best advice I can give a contract coder is to first, possess excellent coding skills and apply them in a consistent manner."
—Susan Brown, ART

Becoming an entrepreneur does not have to occur suddenly or traumatically. Rushing head-on into the unknowns of owning and running your own business is not necessary and is not something we advise. First of all, there are many references and resources that you can refer to for insight before you make the final decision to go it alone. Then there are a variety of things you can do. You can start your contracting "on the side" while continuing to draw a salary from a job you hold, so that you have an opportunity to test the viability of a contract service before you burn any bridges behind you. Chances are you've already done coding in other facilities to help with backlogs as a contingent employee. With this book we've given you the tool to change the format by working in your own business with all the added rewards and challenges that come with it.

You should develop a personal style that works best for you, develop your own plan of action and move forward. All business people who survive and succeed learn to be flexible, to make personal and professional changes when necessary. When you make a mistake or discover an area of business that is not working for you, accept the situation and make necessary corrections to solve the problems and keep you progressing. You can use some of the ideas presented in this book immediately. Others you will modify, reserve for later use, or discard. Ultimately, you must develop your own plan, one that is tailored to meet your unique personal business requirements.

Individuals who have the self-confidence as well as the initiative to take the leap into self-employment are usually people who are willing to give 100% of themselves. Such commitment is revealed in your attitude toward life as well as in your job performance. That's what prospective clients are looking for ... and what they are willing to pay for.

TRANSITIONING INTO A CONSULTING CAREER

Consulting activities usually fall into three categories: providing assistance, providing advice and/or providing information.

Many people rule out careers in consulting because they feel that they must be proficient and an expert in all aspects of a career. The consultant vs. employee merely develops the way in which he or she delivers services. Coding is your area of expertise and you will be looking for opportunities of employment requiring that specific skill.

Consulting is not a profession but a way of practicing a profession. Coding is one of a variety of opportunities for consultants in health care. You may work as either an internal or an external consultant.

Acting as an external consultant, you might be hired on an engagement-by-engagement basis to perform coding tasks.

As a consultant you will face a variety of challenges, some days working on projects at home, other days traveling through airports and on the road, speaking with prospective clients and more.

ESTABLISHING PRIORITIES

Coders who are successful at self-employment are those who are aware of and prepared for the more difficult side of independence. Being on your own is not all fun and games, and not everyone is suited to the challenge. To determine if you are a likely candidate for an independent coding career, you must carefully examine your goals, skills, schedule, commitment and lifestyle.

What do you desire to accomplish? Will your commitment be a part-time venture — two, four, six hours a day, a few days a week — or are you planning on doing this full-time, *at least* forty hours per week? Planning future work hours may be difficult to project if you are new at freelancing, but it is important to know your professional capabilities. As your client base grows and your management responsibilities increase, knowing your coding limits, i.e., level of expertise, per chart, per hour, etc. will be very important revenue production factors.

FACILITY REQUIREMENTS

Each facility will have its own requirements or tasks for the contract coder to follow. Some facilities may require completion of QA data or manual abstracting for the records; others may require that the coder directly abstract into the computer while coding. Some facilities will pull the records and have them available when the coder arrives; others will have the coder retrieve the records.

DEVELOPING GOOD WORKING RELATIONSHIPS

Working relationships will vary from facility to facility but try to develop and maintain positive relationships with the employees whenever possible. Make every effort to establish a good working relationship with the in-house coders. They play a major role in determining your continuing contract.

ADVICE FROM AN EXPERT

Susan Brown, ART, states, "The best advice I can give a contract coder is to first, possess excellent coding skills and apply them in a consistent manner. Second, while you have to deal with managers, you must work with in-house coders. In-house coders have a great deal of impact on the continuation of your contract and repeat business. Developing a good relationship with them is essential. You may be an expert, but it is best if you let them discover that on their own."

A simple statement such as "I'm a coder just like you. I just happen to do it on the road," worked into a conversation within the first couple of days of a new contract will work wonders. It will help dispel any feelings of resentment and you will be welcomed as a helpmate rather than viewed as a threat.

Remember to focus on the work at hand while maintaining ethical conduct and avoiding office politics. By doing so you will improve your professional relationships and increase your productivity.

GETTING AND RETAINING CLIENTS

SELECTING CLIENTS

Often, the greatest and most feared challenge for new business owners and consultants is marketing their services to potential clients. Joining organizations and attending meetings and seminars will enable you to network with peers, and also affords you an opportunity to distribute your business cards whenever appropriate. This can eliminate costly advertising that often does not yield a satisfactory return in business.

MOONLIGHTING —
DON'T QUIT THAT DAY JOB JUST YET!

Few businesses start out making high earnings, even though some industrious, high-volume producers can accomplish this with good luck and a lot of hard work. Many businesses have been launched through moonlighting, and this may be the ideal way for you to test your coding independence. Hanging onto your job while you are testing the waters is a wise decision. Regular paychecks can help you avoid the sink-or-swim feeling you may get while building your independent business. This also allows you to feed your family while you are developing and expanding your business. As you increase your volume you will be able to eventually wean yourself from that job. However, if in the course of moonlighting you discover that you are a low volume producer — which may occur for a variety of personal and professional reasons — you may decide that self-employment will not be suitable for you. You may be glad you still have that day job!

You might also want to consider working for another coding contract service that utilizes independent contract coders. For many independent coders, this is an excellent choice while establishing your business. Advantages include flexibility and a steady income. Also important, working for a service can be a great learning experience, enabling you to see how a contract service functions, allowing you to become oriented with the work environment, and giving you an edge over less experienced coders breaking into the field.

One disadvantage may be contract clauses that prevent you from entering into your own contract with any of the services' clients. And, if you choose this route you will most likely be traveling to various facilities, which, depending on your point of view, may be an advantage or a disadvantage.

BUSINESS ETHICS

*Ethics: A system of moral standards or values; essential
quality; conforming to the standards of
a given group or profession.*

In this country the current reimbursement system has made everyone
increasingly aware and concerned about ethics and the role of
ethical behavior in our business and professional lives. Health
care industry studies indicate that there is an estimated ten billion
dollars in fraudulent annual billing occurring in our industry. Such
astounding and shocking numbers force us to face modern-day billing
reality — health care coding ethics are extremely important. If billing
fraud is to be eliminated or reduced, coders and other affiliated health
care professionals must take action regarding ethical practices,
establishing parameters for what constitutes ethical coding behavior
for reimbursement purposes and helping implement and monitor ethical
coding procedures.

Professional Conduct: Your professional image and attitude as an
independent coder must be credible, and confidentiality of medical
information must be maintained at all times. The coder who is

professional in deed as well as name abides by the professional code of ethics of the American Health Information Management Association, by not participating in illegal or unethical acts, and adheres to pertinent laws and regulations and practices by these standards.

What constitutes ethical behavior? The ethics of coding, as in every profession and business, are built on a solid foundation of moral standards which are applied to coding policies and procedures. These standards include integrity, honesty, competence, respect, fairness, trust and courage. It is the responsibility of coding and health care professionals to establish and adopt ethical policies regarding billing and reimbursement, implement the policies comprehensively, and monitor them consistently, making corrective changes when necessary.

CODING PRINCIPLES

Professional coders abide by the following coding principles:

- Only individuals with appropriate background and training should engage in the coding function.

- Ongoing training and acquiring continuing education units (CEU) is necessary on an annual basis.

- Coding is governed by national guidelines established for the particular setting in which the coding function is performed.

- Coding is governed by state law where applicable.

- Only code information is documented in the medical record.

- Avoiding unethical coding practices.

WHERE TO ASK FOR HELP

When coding questions arise, an excellent resource is the Central Office on ICD-9-CM, the American Hospital Association. Note: *The Central Office provides coding advice at no additional charge to subscribers of Coding Clinic, American Hospital Association or its affiliates.*

Coding Advice
Central Office on ICD-9-CM
American Hospital Association
One North Franklin
Chicago, Il 60606

UNETHICAL CODING

Fraud is a deception deliberately practiced to secure unfair or unlawful gain. If there is a concern about unethical coding, or the use of an incorrect code to unlawfully increase reimbursement, you must determine several things:

1) Is the medical record being incorrectly or incompletely documented to obtain a higher reimbursement?

2) Can you show where a condition is being coded that does not exist?

3) Is a code used to conceal a condition or procedure that is not covered?

If you find yourself in a situation where coding practices are in question you can take the following steps:

- Define and document the coding issue. Use a coding reference such as Coding Clinic to define the issue.

- Share the rule or coding guideline with the client.

- Obtain written advice from an official source such as ICD-9 and HCPCs.

- Document the situation in a memo to the client; include the current date and define the problem, including the coding reference and the impact on reimbursement. Attach supporting documentation. Provide a copy of a portion of the patient's record that illustrates your position, or review these documents with your client. (Keep a copy of this correspondence for your records.)

The American Health Information Management Association (AHIMA) expects its members live up to certain standards of conduct, as documented in the AHIMA Code of Ethical Conduct. These include Point #1: Health information management professionals respect the rights and dignity of all individuals; and Point #5: Health information management professionals accept the responsibility to protect the public and the profession from unethical, incompetent, or illegal acts. (To read AHIMA's complete Code of Ethical Conduct, see the appendix of this book.)

Every professional has an ethical responsibility to refuse to participate in fraudulent activities.

ETHICS IN THE DRG SYSTEM

In the DRG system the following are examples of unethical or illegal coding practices:

- Coding the principal diagnosis incorrectly so that the case will fall into the higher paying Mechanical Ventilator DRG.

- Coding conditions which are not relevant to the hospital stay such as chronic urinary tract infection when the documentation does not support this as a treated relevant problem.

ETHICS IN THE CPT SYSTEM

In the CPT System the following are examples of unethical or illegal coding practices:

- Coding procedures on the ASC (Ambulatory Surgery Center) list in order to get paid, when a procedure not on the list is truly performed

- Coding procedures not on the ASC list when they are not performed in order to increase reimbursement

- Unbundling the services provided into separate CPT codes, when one code is available

OTHER CODING CONCERNS

Unethical coding may include the following:

- Failure to code a relevant condition or complication when it is documented in the medical record

- Coding a service in order for it to be covered when it should not be covered

●Coding another condition as the principal diagnosis when the patient's treatment is directed towards a diagnosis with a lower paying DRG

Ethical coding policies must be followed at all times. This includes the correct choice of principal diagnosis and procedures with resultant DRG regardless of reimbursement assignments. Making a commitment to coding in an ethical fashion is not always an easy task, but as health information professionals it is our responsibility.

And, last but not least, ethics is basically an issue of fairness. Balance priorities, consider other people's concerns as well as economic concerns. Balance your natural self-interest with the interests of others. Know when to put aside selfish, personal needs and act on the behalf of the welfare of many people.

OPTIMIZATION THROUGH QUALITY CODING

The responsibility of the coding professional is to achieve and maintain quality coding data, regardless of the financial outcome. Ethics enter into any coding related function whether it be auditing for revenue enhancement, cost containment or coding of daily discharges. The coder must strive to achieve great performance while abiding by ethical standards. Since the onset of DRGs in 1983, increased emphasis has been placed on coding for reimbursement.

Many of these reimbursement systems are code-based and utilize ICD-9-CM and/or CPT-4. They include the following:

●Ambulatory Patient Groups (APGs)
●Ambulatory Surgery Center (ASCs)
●Resource-Based Relative Value Scales (RBRVS)

There are several terms that define various reimbursement strategies and that state the use and purpose of :

- •Maximize: Raise to highest degree possible

- •Minimize: Reduce to the least possible degree or amount

- •Optimize: Make the most of; develop or realize to the utmost extent; obtain the most efficient or optimum use of.

Optimization is achieved by having sufficient knowledge of the Prospective Payment System to confirm the DRG assignment which ensures optimal reimbursement. The reality in inpatient coding today is that when dealing with patients reimbursed on a DRG basis, we are responsible for ensuring that our employer receives the maximum allowable reimbursement which is available under current coding guideline environment.

Reimbursement is optimized by appropriate assignment of diagnostic and procedure codes. The task of "right-coding", i.e., optimizing, is a very difficult one and often leads to other reimbursement strategies such as "upcoding", i.e., maximizing (reimbursement increased by inaccurate selection of a code), or "downcoding", i.e., minimizing (reimbursement is decreased by inappropriate assignment of code). The negative impact of maximizing or minimizing on data integrity, as well as the ethical concerns, are the same.

The strategy for DRG optimization is as follows:

- •Review the medical record for documentation to support a higher resource intensity diagnosis as principal diagnosis.

- •Review the medical record for documentation of the surgeries performed.

- Review the medical record to identify coexisting chronic conditions which have been exacerbated or required treatment with medications or monitoring or are a risk factor for the patient's treatment.

- Review the medical record to identify transient conditions which require treatment during the hospital stay.

Coding will play a significant role in determining health care in the future, from reimbursement to quality-of-care issues. It is crucial that coding functions be performed in accordance with ICD-9-CM and CPT-4 coding guidelines, supported by precise physician documentation; and it is essential for the coder to perform his/her function with integrity. Appropriate optimization will allow for appropriate reimbursement. Accurate coding is crucial to the development of new data systems which are based on the statistical data of the systems now in place.

DRG OPTIMIZATION

According to William Haik, M.D., FCCP, director of DRG Review in Fort Walton Beach, FL, the purpose of the DRG system is to maintain budget neutrality (for Medicare) without having the budget. DRG revisions are driven by Congress and how it allocates the federal budget. It is very important to receive current updates on DRG changes because they could potentially have an impact on reimbursement increases (or decreases).

DRG optimization is the utilization of all legitimate resources available to maximize reimbursement to the facility for all services given in all cases of medial diagnoses, procedures and treatment.

An extensive background in DRG optimization is essential if you are considering any form of DRG contracting. For this level of coding, a complete understanding of the medical record is of utmost importance. In addition, you must be comfortable with those occasions when you will need to educate physicians, nurses and other health care professionals regarding correct coding and its importance. You will wear many hats if you are considering contracting for DRGs.

The basic service you can provide is as follows:

- Clinical review of the medical record from admission to discharge.

- Improvements are noted for each medical record in the specific location that will fit on a work sheet. (See appendix for work sheet example.) The work sheet contains all identifying information, hospital assigned DRG, ICD-9-CM codes, procedure codes, principal diagnoses and secondary diagnoses. Recommended improvements are made by the consultant, specific locations where improvements are found (such as history, emergency room, operative report, pathology, x-ray, electrocardiogram, etc.) which may increase reimbursement and/or for coding education. Recommended improvements are discussed at the bottom of each work sheet using the logic as well as the clinical analysis leading to the DRG change.

After each audit a summary of all medical records reviewed and/or changes are submitted to the health information manager. At the end of the month confirmed DRG changes that are agreed/disagreed to are returned. The percent or fee agreed upon by contract is forwarded to the facility's finance department. Fees are usually based upon a percentage of the increase in the DRG payment. Example: the original

DRG pays $2,000; after review it is increased to $3,000. The increase is $1,000. If your percentage is 50% you will be paid $500 for your service.

WHEN NOT TO CODE

Every professional coder knows that quality coding depends on quality documentation. Whether coding inpatient or outpatient records, the diagnosis and/or procedure codes chosen must come from the information contained in the medical record. If the medical record does not include appropriate documentation, the codes assigned will not accurately reflect services provided. In many cases this impacts financial reimbursement.

Unfortunately, clinicians who are responsible for data quality do not always supply it. One primary reason is that they may not understand the need for data quality. Often, health information professionals must take an active role in educating physicians, nurses and other health care professionals on the importance of an accurate, comprehensive medical record.

Should you code without the following reports? You Decide.

Discharge Summary: Often, the discharge summary is not available at the time of coding. If it is available, great! If not, use other resources such as the death certificate.

H&P (History and Physical Examination): A current history and physical examination should be available to code a record completely and accurately.

OP/Pathology Report: The operative report has information documented that can rarely be retrieved from other documents in the medical record. The pathology report is essential for accurate coding. Surgeons may indicate that it looks like normal tissue and the diagnosis may change after the pathologist examines the specimen. If possible, don't proceed with coding until the pathologist's report is available (this can be a reasonable time-frame agreed upon by you and your client). If tissue is sent out for further analysis, ask the director for her requirements.

DOCUMENTATION CONCERNS

When you have questions or concerns, ask for more information, and don't be afraid to ask for reports that are needed. Use good judgment and **always remember to document which report is not available at the time you are coding the chart**.

Quality should be the underlying goal for your business. Work swiftly but accurately, and return charts as required. This procedure will save you time and money, since charts noted to be incomplete or incorrect will be returned to you.

RISK MANAGEMENT / QUALITY IMPROVEMENT

"Quality is the frosting on the cake of good business."

The quest for quality has driven businesses to relentlessly examine their operations and continuously improve their products and services. Even in light of this driven intent, programs will not succeed without motivated, quality-conscious people. In your business, this starts with you! You are the most important person in quality improvement. Unless there is a commitment and concerted effort from you, the push for excellence will not make it past the starting line.

Keep commitments: Make sure you follow-through with your commitments. The work may not be there tomorrow. Failing to follow through with commitments can be costly. To earn respect you must deliver.

Set performance goals: Decide how to meet your goals and release only acceptable work.

Stay visible: Keep in touch with your clients. Follow-up is critical.

Keep customers satisfied: Seventy-five percent of dissatisfied customers will do business with a company again — if their complaints are resolved. Express concern and follow up.

Maintain telephone power: Be sure to respond to phone messages in a timely manner.

Attain and maintain organizational excellence: Prepare an action plan and organize your personal and professional life.

Ken Blanchard, author of *The One Minute Manager*, lists four fundamental elements that will help attain personal and organization excellence:

- Goal setting — Write down clear objectives.

- Commitment — Dedicate yourself to achieving your goals.

- Feedback — You must get feedback to determine if you are moving in the right direction. There must be a built-in system for tracking performance.

- Organizational support — This may include family and friends who coach and encourage you.

MAINTAINING CONFIDENTIALITY

As health care professionals, no matter what work setting, we have a solemn duty to uphold a patient's right to privacy, and to assure that information contained in the patient record will NOT BE DISCLOSED inside or outside the health care facility.

Failure to appropriately protect a patient's privacy may result in fines or lawsuits. State and federal laws specify what information may be released. We have a legal and moral duty not to pry and not to disclose information about patients, doctors or other health care workers. We must also be alert to inappropriate access by others or inappropriate sharing of information. Security begins when the patient is first seen for treatment, and it should never end.

CONFIDENTIALITY AND HOME-BASED CODING

Although most health care professionals agree that coding at home is likely to increase productivity, reduce turnover and boost recruiting efforts, some express concerns about confidentiality of patient records, fearful the delicate information may not be kept secure. They need not fear. When taking proper precautions to protect patient information is a priority, patient information is as secure in the coder's home as it is in the hospital. Home-based coders should always be prepared to explain their standard procedures for maintaining confidential records and reassure clients that information will be protected.

- Keep your records in a secure place and do not leave them unattended.

- Observe all appropriate laws for handling release of information.

- Don't indulge in informal chats or make comments about details of a patient's condition or care — not in your office, on the phone or online. Avoid the temptation to discuss, even anonymously, that humorous or unbelievable case.

- When you must discuss medical information, e.g., to get help in coding a case, do so quietly and in a private manner.

- Always be alert to the potential for accidental disclosure of confidential information.

- Don't leave documents such as surgery schedules or other patient lists in places that are accessible to others.

- Don't leave medical reports or records open on your desk when you are not using them; others near might accidentally see data that they should not see.

- Ensure that your computer terminals cannot be easily read by visitors.

- Don't put copies of reports in the trash. Use a designated "shredding box" instead.

- Remember to protect others' confidential information the way you would want your own medical information protected.

THE CONFIDENTIALITY STATEMENT

Home-based coders are now required to sign a confidentiality statement, and, because the home-based coder is transporting records, this confidentiality statement is often more detailed than those in-house coders are required to sign. Your policy should reflect the precautions you take when transporting paper records, i.e., in a closed bag during transport and that your coding office is in a private area of the home with an area to lock up records.

Computer security should be addressed, with entry into the system only through a password before gaining access to the hospital's system. Most hospital security systems have a log-out time, which means that if the coder does not touch the keyboard for five minutes, the system automatically logs off so that patient information is no longer displayed on the screen. This combination of built-in technical security, access levels and education helps to keep patient information secure.

FAXING HEALTH CARE DOCUMENTS

If you occasionally fax documents, be sure to include a disclaimer on the cover sheet warning the recipient not to read the document if it has been received in error.

ONLINE INFORMATION SECURITY

The World Wide Web has made it fairly easy for people to access information, and medical data is a hot item. Even communications with physicians can be readily accessed. Unfortunately, there is a lack of anonymity associated with online use, and there are individuals who have found ways to monitor web sites and chat rooms, and in some cases information swapping is also a hot black marketing item. Online privacy is an issue that is being debated in Washington, and through Federal Trade Commission (FTC) hearings. With the government's involvement in online privacy issues, new legislation may eventually evolve, but no one knows if even that will be adequate. Technology changes so rapidly that by the time a monitoring or controlling mechanism is in place, newer, more sophisticated technological challenges have already appeared.

The American Health Information Management Association (AHIMA) is an active participant in the issues surrounding online privacy and has developed its own guidelines for online privacy.

ETHICS AND RISK MANAGEMENT FOR OUTPATIENT CODERS

Professional ethics are a must. Outpatient coders/billers are bound by the same rules of confidentiality regarding patient information that any other health care provider is, including the billing department. No information, including financial information, is to be released without a signed record release from the patient. Confidential information cannot be given to another family member without written authorization from the patient.

As a coder/biller you must be totally honest, ethical, aboveboard and credible, because you are dealing with the practice's life blood. The relationship must be a two-way street. If you feel that a practice is not being honest with you, cut them loose. If they are not willing to pay you for your services, fire them. Keep copies of your coding logs and recovery logs. When you bill your clients, provide a copy to them but let them know that you also hold a copy. You become the gatekeeper.

Frequently in the outpatient coding arena, physicians are so fearful that their practices will suffer or be lost that up to 90% of reports are undercoded instead of upcoded.

The demand for outpatient coding/billing services has increased because it takes a tremendous burden off the practice to have a qualified professional coding specialist managing the coding/billing. If you find yourself in this situation, be prepared to be patient. For many physicians, this is a new venture and others have had more than one traumatic experience with billing services. So, for the first three months or so, your new client may telephone almost every day, consulting with you for clarification of codes and seeking documentation advice. It is important that you work with each doctor until he or she develops confidence and trust in your work.

BEWARE OF "BILLING IN A BOX"

Billing software programs are being marketed aggressively. They are promoted as perhaps the only investment required to launch you into a medical billing career. Sometimes, the training provides only a few hours of coding education and then leaves you on your own to find clients. You have probably seen billing-in-a-box advertising in the classified sections at the back of magazines under an enticing heading such as "learn medical billing at home." Such programs are not always what they seem to be, so check them out to avoid disappointment. Also, some in the medical community view them with skepticism.

RISK MANAGEMENT AND PROFESSIONAL LIABILITY

A business liability policy will help protect you in the event that data is lost during its transition from the doctor's office. (This issue should also be addressed in the client contract waiver.)

> *"As a coder/biller you must be totally honest, ethical, aboveboard and credible."*

157

KEEPING RECORDS

Working independently means that you are responsible not just for providing a service, but for keeping your own records — **high quality records**. Accurate record keeping will help you avoid many pitfalls with the IRS and other regulating bodies. Retention of business records is extremely important for IRS purposes.

- Copies of all contracts
- Lists of services that you provide your clients
- Rate and fee schedule
- Coverage arrangements
- Confidentiality contracts
- Liability coverage
- Records of all work done each day — by client or production
- Records of any corrections
- A copy of the written record or coding guideline provided by the contracting hospital or client

Some recommended record retention schedules include the following:

- Payment records, 7 years
- Bank statements, 3 years
- Expired contracts, 7 years
- General correspondence, 2 years
- Canceled checks, permanently
- Financial statements, permanently
- Tax returns and work sheets, permanently

CODING—
DAILY LOG SHEETS/AUDIT CONTROL OF WORK FLOW

We recommend you maintain the following information/documents:

- A daily log showing the number of charts coded

- Discharge types — inpatient, outpatient surgery, transitional care, emergency room, outpatient laboratory data, etc.

- Insurance types — Medicare vs. non-Medicare, Medi-Cal (additional CPT coding needed)

- Complicated cases — long "length of stay", multiple procedures, etc.

- Excessively delayed computer response time or unexpected down time

- Time spent answering questions or helping a physician, another coder or other health care professional

- Unusual situations or tasks that are time-consuming

THE INDEPENDENT CONTRACTOR

Independent Contractor

*A person hired to perform a service with responsibility for the
end results of the effort. The hirer has no control
over the independent contractor's methods
of performance or details of work
such as one would haveover
an employee's labor.*

On the surface, the definition of an independent contractor seems simple, but in working-world reality, it is actually quite complex. Our government has established very specific rules and regulations regarding who and who cannot legally call themselves independent contractors. Even with rules, however, there are gray areas, and some "independent contractors" have found themselves in hot water. Others, of course, are in trouble because they have made no attempt whatever to follow the rules. Don't let this happen to you.

Anyone desiring to be an independent contractor should clearly understand the following four points:

1. Government rules determine if a worker is an independent contractor. The IRS and state laws determine whether a worker is an independent contractor or an employee — *not the written or oral agreements between you and the person you contract with*. A contract in a file is not proof of an independent contractor relationship.

2. Workers are employees unless the hiring firm can prove otherwise.

3. Independent contractor status has nothing to do with job titles or type of work. Two people can do exactly the same job. One can be a true independent contractor, and the other can be an employee. It all depends upon how the hiring firm treats each worker.

4. One mistake can cause an independent contractor to be converted into employee status. Independent contractor status is not static. Any action by the hiring firm or its employees to control independent contractors can convert them into employees.

Court decisions or legislation may significantly alter the validity of this information. It is wise to periodically consult an attorney or other tax professional who monitors independent contractor rulings.

The key issue in determining whether or not a worker is an independent contractor is this: Who has the right to control the worker and how the work is accomplished. If a hiring firm controls the means by which work is done, the worker is automatically an employee. If the hiring firm can exercise control only on results of the work, the worker can be an independent contractor. It is important to remember that it is the right to control, not the actual exercising of control, that is important. The hiring firm cannot control an independent contractor's work. If it does, the legal status will automatically be an employer-employee relationship and the hiring firm will be liable for employment taxes and benefits. What can the hiring firm do? It has the right to exercise control over the independent contractor as to the results of the work, and it can provide job specifications to the independent contractor.

A hiring firm can only terminate an independent contractor if he or she breaches the contract or if completed work is unacceptable. If a hiring firm claims the right to fire a worker at will, the worker's legal status usually is an employee.

For more information, research other business publications, the Internet, tax guides and legal references which review and keep current on facts and issues surrounding independent contractor status.

BENEFITS TO INDEPENDENT CONTRACTORS

Independent contractors enjoy many personal and professional benefits, including the following.

- Personal flexibility

- Being your own boss

- Tax-deductible business expenses

- Continuing education and experience in managing and operating your own business

- Opportunity to expand your horizons and diversify

RISKS TO INDEPENDENT CONTRACTORS

Those interested in going solo should also consider the risks independent contractors face:

- No disability or workers' compensation insurance

- No unemployment insurance

- Potential liability for professional actions

- Potential tax troubles

- Potential failure

INDEPENDENT CONTRACTING AND THE TWENTY COMMON LAW PRINCIPLES

When the IRS audits a company and spot-checks for fraudulent independent contractors, it relies on these twenty "common law" principles:

1. **No Instructions**
   Contractors cannot be required to follow step-by-step instructions to accomplish their tasks. (*They can follow job specifications, however.*)

2. **No Training**
   Contractors rarely receive training from clients to perform a task.

3. **Service can be rendered by others**
   Contractors can hire others to do the work for them.

4. **Own work hours**
Contractors set their own work hours.

5. **Nonessential work**
Contract work is not essential to the company. (*The company does not rely solely on the contractor for its survival.*)

6. **No day-to-day working relationship**
Most contractors do not have a day-to-day relationship with their clients.

7. **Control of assistants**
Contractors can hire, supervise and pay assistants independent of their clients.

8. **Time to pursue other work**
Contractors should have enough time to pursue other work.

9. **Job location**
The contractor decides when and where the work is done. (*Even though coding is often done on-site, the coder still makes this decision.*)

10. **Order of work set**
The contractor has control of the sequence of tasks that lead to finishing the job.

11. **No progress reports**
Contractors are not required to submit interim reports to clients.

12. **Paid for the job**
Contractors are paid for the job, not for the time spent doing the job.

13. **Working for multiple firms**
Contractors should have time to do work for more than one client.

14. **Business expenses**
In most cases, contractors should pay their own expenses involved in doing a job. (*Expenses for travel and lodging may be negotiated into a contract agreement if the work requires extensive travel, as is often the case with coding.*)

15. **Own tools**
Contractors should furnish their own tools. (*Coders usually have their own reference books and laptop computers.*)

16. **Significant investment**
Contractors' investment in their trade must be significant enough to make them independent of client's facilities.

17. **Services available to the public**
Contractors must show they make their services available to other clients.

18. **Potential profit or loss**
Contractors are liable for any expenses and liabilities they may encounter in performing their jobs.

19. **Limited right to discharge**
Contractors cannot be fired at will so long as they produce a result specified in their contract.

20. **No compensation for noncompletion**
Contractors cannot be paid for partial completion of a job.

Failure to satisfy all 20 principles may result in an Internal Revenue Service audit on the past three years with the business owner penalized for each misclassified worker, whether they were deliberately misclassified or the misclassification resulted from an honest mistake. One mistake can easily cost a business $25,000.

The 20 common law factors described above were developed by the IRS; however, there are other government agencies that determine whether workers are independent contractors or employees. These governing agencies will vary from state to state.

Like the IRS, all these agencies consistently agree upon one key determining factor: In a true independent contractor relationship, the hiring firm has no right to control the work of the worker.

However, each agency has developed its own "factor list" to show right to control. For the most part they parallel the IRS factors. Here are the most important factors common to all these agencies:

1. Hiring firm does not have the right to control the worker

2. Type of work is not the hiring firm's primary business

3. It is not a continuing relationship

4. Payment is made by the job

5. Worker has own tools

6. Worker cannot be fired at will

7. Worker determines job location

8. Worker has a distinct occupation or operates a separate business

SIX FACTOR "ECONOMIC REALITIES" TEST

The U. S. Department of Labor uses a six point "Economic Realities" test to determine if a worker is an independent contractor. Reference: *Employment Relationship Under the Fair Labor Standards Act*, Publication 1297, U. S. Department of Labor.

1. Work should not be part of the hiring firm's regular business

2. Working relationship should have a degree of non-permanence

3. Worker should have invested in equipment, materials, or assistants

4. Hiring firm should have no right to control work

5. Opportunity for profit or loss exists, depending on the worker's managerial skills

6. Work should require initiative, judgment, or foresight to successfully compete with others

THE REALITY CHECK

You must look at **all 20 common law factors**. Do not rely on any one factor. Aside from determining which factors are the most important, examine the factors that you cannot meet and ask yourself why. Work on meeting all those factors before you call yourself an independent contractor.

Give yourself a reality check. You must be willing and able to do the following:

- Be an entrepreneur and take business risks (make a profit or loss on jobs)

- Assume liability if the work is faulty

- Hire assistants

- Invest in your business

- Advertise

- Be able to conduct business even after losing a client

If you are not willing to do that, then you cannot classify yourself as an independent contractor.

SUBCONTRACTING

Working as a consulting firm employee can be a great help in developing your coding consultant career, easing you through many of the requirements we have discussed earlier in this book. By starting out as an employee of an already established coding/consulting firm, you will learn much about coding and consulting. These companies often provide training on and off the job site and will usually provide you with the current regulations and other publications needed to stay current in your field. There may also be some benefits and travel allowances. This is a comfortable way to take your first step into consulting, and through it, decide if you would really like being an independent. If so, when the time comes and you feel ready, you can then begin working on your own.

Subcontracting to an established medical record coding/consultant company is another alternative for you as an independent coder. Check out news magazines for health information professionals and the Internet for companies advertising their need for coding specialists.

There is a wide range of coding support positions available in the marketplace. Do some research, take a look at potential opportunities appropriate for your background, and market yourself accordingly.

Coding/consultant companies have already established a subcontract wage range around which they are willing to negotiate. It might be an hourly agreement or perhaps a dollar amount per type of service rendered. Depending on the type of coding or service you will be providing, your contract wages will fluctuate. These companies are also very aware of independents' increase-in-salary needs for travel expenses, insurance needs, tax reporting requirements, etc. (Because of the myriad variations in the coding field, we recommend you refer to the chapter on "doing your homework" before negotiating your fees.) In most situations, reputable companies are fair in contract wages offered. They have a vested interest, for they know that having a good working relationship with you will enhance their company's image because you will be representing the services they provide.

Generally, each coding/consulting company provides software based on what services their company offers. From personal experience, we recommend that you keep that old (but always updated!) code book at your side. If you don't already, you will come to depend on that valuable reference material.

Learning to be a savvy independent never hurts! If you maintain a professional and ethical attitude throughout your first contract, you will find that future negotiations with clients and contractors will be easier.

Staying up-to-date and informed will add to your success. Being knowledgeable and keeping on top of the market you are entering will give you more power! It's a wise idea to keep tickler files for new software, salary outlooks, books (like this one), coding changes and updates, area needs, future projections for the profession, and new companies and potential competition. To be successful you must be constantly aware of the challenges and changes in the industry. Listen, read, educate, learn.

ASSISTANCE FROM THE CHAMBER OF COMMERCE

In California there is an Independent Contractor Package designed to make it easier for independent contractors to comply with government requirements and plan for unexpected illnesses, injuries, or unemployment. This package is available through the state chamber of commerce and through some local chambers.

The California Chamber of Commerce
P. O. Box 1736
Sacramento, CA 95812-1736
916-444-6670

For those outside California, locate your state's chamber of commerce in the resource section at the back of this book. Contact your state's chamber of commerce to see what resources they offer small businesses.

NECESSARY DOCUMENTS

Have the appropriate documents in order. To protect itself, a hiring firm may ask you for the following items:

1. Contractor's business license

2. Contractor's fictitious name statement (if applicable)

3. Evidence of insurance (business liability coverage)

ADDITIONAL REFERENCE MATERIALS

In addition to the books and forms for sale in book stores, numerous free or low cost reference materials are available through your local library and government offices. You can order publications from the Internal Revenue Service (IRS), the Small Business Administration (SBA), the Department of Commerce, and your state resources offer an extensive selection of information on most business management topics. All of this information is listed in *The Small Business Directory*. For a free copy write to SBA Publications.

SBA Publications
P. O. Box 1000
Fort Worth, TX 76119

FINANCES

"First and foremost, you must manage your finances."

Setting up an independent health care coding business requires an investment of time and money. In the beginning, your dollar investment need not be great, but it must be managed well if you want your business to survive. As your business grows, consistent and regular money management will bring you not only economic success, but professional respect, too. It is important to learn how to consistently manage your finances.

FINANCIAL NEEDS AND CAPITAL INVESTMENT

A home-based business can be established with little or no start-up capital. Your business is a labor intensive business — you provide a service. Initially you will need only a modest monetary investment in facilities and equipment. The greater investment will be the labor involved; that is, the service you offer which you will personally provide.

You will need little in the way of office facilities, and you may provide your services in facilities provided by your clients — on-site, on the client's premises — where you have free access to computers, copying machines and other equipment.

Perhaps you have enough personal working capital to get started on a modest scale, but you may soon find that you do not have enough operating capital to pay expenses right away or draw even a modest salary while your business is growing. This is a cash flow problem to avoid if possible.

Financial experts report that many entrepreneurs do not recognize the need for up-front operating capital. They naively assume that income will begin to flow as soon as they begin working at their chosen business. There are two serious flaws to this line of reasoning:

1. **Your business may not start with a rush.** Most new businesses get off to a slow start. It usually takes time to develop business to the point where income exceeds expenses. This is especially true for a home-based venture.

2. **Cash may not flow in immediately.** Even if you acquire clients quickly and business is very good, it will still take some time for collections, or cash inflow. It depends on your billing practices and the length of time it takes clients to pay. Let's assume you bill on the first of each month.

If you start your account on the 10th of the month, you will work 20 days before you can bill, and the client will likely take another 15 or more days to pay the bill. On a full month, from the date the billing period starts until the time you receive payment could be 45 or more days.

Some of your clients may deliberately delay payment to you to enhance their cash flow. Soon, you may have a great deal of "billed out" money owed to you ("accounts receivable"). You need to collect that cash in order to pay your bills.

Instead of using personal savings, you may choose to take out a loan to get started. Do a monthly cash flow projection to forecast the cash you expect to receive and disburse during your first year or two.

WATCH YOUR COSTS AND EXPENSES

Cost reduction is important and cost avoidance even better, especially for a start-up business. The typical mistakes made by many novices are understandable.

You start out in business with enthusiasm, cheered on by friends and relatives. With this solid base of self-assurance and confidence, you begin with great style: handsome new furniture, shiny new equipment, expensive stationery, loads of office supplies, and a few extra goodies you could not resist. Almost all of this expense is not necessary!

You can do as much business at a secondhand or homemade desk, using modest stationery. A computer with packaged office software and a fax machine will function very nicely in your home office.

USING A BUSINESS CREDIT CARD

I don't know about you, but every year at tax time I find myself inundated with little bits and pieces of paper detailing my business expenses. Well, I have found the perfect solution . . . the American Express Gold Card.

Two years ago, AMEX began offering its customers an end-of-year summary, detailing all transactions made on the card per year by categories, i.e., airline, travel, restaurant, merchandise, service fees, entertainment, health related, etc. I made the decision at that time to use this card only for business expenses. Oh, I still save all my receipts, but at the end of the year when I'm gathering and organizing financial data, it's so much easier to refer to my AMEX summary for itemizing tax deductions. Since almost all businesses accept the AMEX card, it is a very easy way to keep track of business expenses.

The annual fee for the AMEX card is $75/year, which is quite a bargain when you consider all the time spent, and time saved, getting paperwork ready for your accountant.

One special benefit to AMEX card users is a warranty extension on equipment. When using the AMEX card for equipment purchases, the company will double the warranty agreement. For instance, if you used your AMEX card to purchase a computer which came with a one year warranty, AMEX would extend the warranty for another year so the equipment would be covered for two years.

There is one major drawback in using the AMEX card, however. You must pay all charges as they are billed. There are no monthly installments. Therefore, before making any purchase, you must make sure you will have money in your business account to cover that expense when it becomes due and payable the following month. For more information regarding the credit card, call American Express.

American Express
800-635-5955

176

EQUIPMENT —
LEASING OR RENTING VERSUS BUYING

You can rent most equipment needed for a business including computers, printers, modems, copiers, or fax machines. The rental agreement may be for a period as short as a single day or for a year or more. If your need for computer equipment is short-term, it usually costs far less to rent than to buy.

Renting can serve as a low-cost way of sampling various pieces of equipment. If you are unsure about the features you need in a computer system, fax machine or copier, short-term renting is a good way to evaluate new or different technologies. If you need to upgrade your equipment within the first year of business, renting will probably offer greater flexibility to acquire equipment.

When starting your business, you may have enough money saved to cover the first three months of your new venture, but that money may be needed for operating expenses — not for purchasing equipment. Even if you want to make an equipment loan from a bank, local bankers may be wary of lending money to your new business.

Rental agencies retain ownership of rented equipment. The renter merely pays for the privilege of using it for a period of time. During the period of the rental agreement, the rental agency is usually obligated to service the equipment if it becomes inoperable. When necessary, the agency is also responsible for replacing the equipment in a timely fashion.

The primary benefits of renting office equipment are conserving up-front cash payment, potential cost savings, and convenience. You pay only for what you use, and may save money by avoiding a large purchase price. Renting should also save time. Rental agencies often have fairly extensive inventories, so they can promptly deliver what you need.

For tax purposes, rental fees, like lease payments, are considered business expenses and are fully tax-deductible. You won't be bothered with complex records of fixed assets and depreciation calculations at tax time.

If you think you will need temporary equipment beyond a few months, determine the most economically advantageous rental period. Monthly payments for personal computer rentals typically hover between 8-11% of the average retail price of the equipment. However, payments can go higher. After eight months to a year of renting, your rental payments will total approximately what you would have paid to buy the system.

Many computer stores offer computer systems for rent. Don't assume that local dealers will be cheaper or more efficient than national chain stores. Prices can vary greatly, so shop for the best bargains.

Don't hesitate to ask questions. Does the quoted price include a complete system? For a computer, will the necessary cables, monitor, video card, or keyboard cost extra? Does the quoted price include delivery and installation of the equipment at the beginning of the rental period and its dismantling and removal when the agreement expires? Does installation service include loading software onto the hard-disk? Does the quoted price include normal maintenance and emergency services?

The level of service offered often differs from vendor to vendor. Do you get prompt on-site service or is the service limited to a technician guiding you through a troubleshooting routine over the telephone?

LEASING EQUIPMENT

When building your business, it is helpful to know how to acquire the equipment you need when you need it. Although you may not have cash or credit to buy equipment outright, you may be able to lease equipment and create an efficient and cost-effective office.

A lease arrangement, with affordable monthly payments applied to the purchase price of equipment, is a viable option for many business owners on a limited budget. At the end of the lease agreement period, the business owner may own the equipment.

Large corporations frequently lease all or part of their office equipment. Among other things, they appreciate the increased flexibility and the convenience of equipment and financing neatly wrapped in one payment package.

The main advantages to leasing equipment are financial. Even though leasing is usually more expensive than buying outright, the ease of tax-deduction from lease expenditures may be more desirable than purchasing and depreciating equipment.

> **NOTE**
>
> *IRS rules and regulations change frequently, so check with your accountant for specific information regarding depreciation.*

Even though you may have ready cash to pay for office needs, leasing offers the advantage of cash conservation. In the beginning, you may need or want to put some of your cash to work in areas that will help generate profit. Instead of buying equipment, you may invest in advertising — business cards, fliers, and space advertising. Leasing allows you to manage cash flow, paying for your equipment over time.

Leasing equipment also gives you a little more leverage with the vendor if a piece of equipment is a "lemon."

In addition, leasing also offers you greater flexibility in terms of payment plans and equipment updates. Because the computer industry is changing at such a rapid pace and new technology is offered with incredible frequency, leasing minimizes your risk of having to use obsolete technology. If your business needs change mid-lease, you may be able to get more powerful equipment with little or no financing penalty. However, this depends on the specific type of lease.

Fixed monthly payments over time represent some savings in real dollars, i.e., your lease payments are made in increasingly devalued (inflated) dollars. In contrast, if you choose to purchase your equipment outright, every dollar you recover through depreciation is worth less due to inflation. Let's look at your leasing options.

- **The closed-end lease, or finance-lease**, allows you to actually purchase the equipment after the last installment has been paid. Generally the purchase price is either a percentage (often 10%) of the original price or a pro forma amount (usually $1). A closed-end lease is nothing more than a disguised loan.

- **An operating lease or open-end lease** offers you three options at the end of the agreement. You can purchase the equipment at its fair market value or at its blue book value. You can renegotiate and extend the lease, usually with new equipment. Or you can simply terminate the lease and the equipment reverts back to the lessor.

You must decide which type lease is best for you. If financing is your primary reason for leasing because you want to eventually own the equipment, the closed-end or finance lease may meet your needs. However, if your goal is to upgrade equipment conveniently and economically, your best bet is the open-end or operating lease. Consult your accountant before making a final decision.

Be aware that you will be paying more by leasing your equipment than by buying it outright. Like credit card loans, you are paying for the privilege of paying over time.

There is a simple formula used by lessors for calculating the monthly cost of a lease, applying a "rate factor" to the purchase price of the equipment. For example, if the rate factor on a three-year finance lease at $5000 were 0.035 or $35 per $1000, monthly payments on this lease would be $175 or five times $35. The rate factor can vary slightly depending on other provisions in the lease, such as payment timing and end-of-lease purchase agreements.

When shopping for a lease, look for one in which the total cost is as close as possible to the equipment's purchase price. Expect to pay a 33% premium if you lease instead of buy.

With a finance lease, shop for the lowest rate factor. To get the maximum benefit from an operating lease, consider the economic life of the equipment and your projected need for equipment upgrades. The ideal operating lease is one whose term actually coincides with the economic life of the leased equipment (the point when the equipment ceases to depreciate any further). At this point you can purchase it at the lowest possible price. If the lease term also corresponds to the "useful life" of the equipment (expiring at just about the time you would be upgrading your equipment), it gives you maximum flexibility in renegotiating the lease for new equipment.

WHEN NOT TO LEASE EQUIPMENT

Internal Revenue Code Section 179 allows immediate deduction for up to $18,500 per year of equipment purchases. With this immediate deduction, you can reduce your income taxes and thereby keep more of your hard-earned cash. Section 179 requires that you use your equipment for five years, so if you plan on trading in your system in three years, you may have to pay the IRS taxes related to the unused portion of the five-year depreciation period. So, generally, you are likely better off purchasing equipment and deducting it under Section 179 instead of leasing the equipment and taking the deduction over the lease period.

In general, leasing makes the most sense when you buy expensive equipment. A $2000 PC won't be worth the effort and expense of setting up a lease agreement. When computers first became affordable for home businesses, the technology was changing rapidly — by the micro-minute it seemed. Just when you thought you had purchased the latest turbo-driven computer, it seemingly became obsolete overnight. Leasing computers at that point made sense. For a very small outlay of cash, a businessperson was able to keep up with expanding technology. Now, however, it is very easy to upgrade computers and it is not hard to keep up with the Jones'. In any case, always check with your tax adviser for advice on purchasing versus leasing in the context of your specific business situation.

There are other situations when leasing might not be a viable equipment option.

- You may not qualify. Some computer equipment lessors want to do business strictly with registered companies, preferably corporations with credit histories, and not with individuals.

- Some leases have riders that prohibit you from moving the equipment out of the state in which you received it. If relocation is a possibility within the next few years, leasing should be avoided.

- A leasing company lien may prevent you from selling the equipment before the lease has expired, even though, with a finance lease, you may eventually own the equipment.

You can't "prepay" a lease. Whereas most bank loans and mortgages allow the borrower to prepay without penalty, with leases you must pay your installments every month whether your business is thriving or floundering. This is generally no great risk to your business, but it is something you should be aware of.

PAYING YOURSELF

As a sole proprietor, how much are your services worth? Well, that depends on your gross receipts. As pointed out earlier in this book, you must save a portion of your gross income to pay such mundane things as self-employment (FICA) taxes, state and federal income taxes, health insurance, disability insurance and all business related expenses. According to most financial experts, your salary could be between 10-45% of your gross receipts. Being home-based medical coders, our overhead is fairly low once the large expenditures for equipment have been made. Therefore our percentage would be greater than that, say, of a building contractor who needs equipment and supplies and may be at the lower end of the pay scale.

Without question, it's tough to figure out your pay when you're self-employed. Take too little from the business and you begin to wonder why you ever kissed off that hospital job and its sweet biweekly paycheck. Take too much and your business may slowly go bust. That's why, according to most financial experts, it is better to err on the side of paying yourself too little. You can always give yourself a bonus at the end of the year.

One way to gauge your pay is to look at the age of your business. Independent medical coders just starting in business shouldn't expect to draw a paycheck from the get-go. Financial experts advise that first-year owners take just enough to cover personal expenses, keeping the remaining revenues for business expenses. In general, it takes six months of steady cash flow — a sign that your business is viable — before you can cut yourself a monthly paycheck.

For service businesses such as ours, a good rule of thumb is to divide gross income into thirds. One-third goes to pay business overhead, one-third goes home, and the other third goes for taxes.

Unfortunately, accounts payables sometimes exceed receivables. Those of us who have been in business for a while understand the fickle nature of medical coding. Come flu season or Joint Commission, we are inundated with work and find ourselves sitting at our computers fourteen hours a day, seven days a week. Then comes summer, and it seems that everyone is on vacation. Always make sure that you have enough cash in the bank to cover expenses in down times.

When money piles up in your account, don't be lulled into thinking you can cut yourself a bigger monthly paycheck. If there's one thing you can always count on, it's unexpected expenses, and a little spare cash may mean the difference between making it through a rocky period or going out of business.

"What is important in life is not the triumph, but the struggle."

TAX INCENTIVES: BUSINESS TAXES

Smart home-based medical coders should learn all they can about different types of business taxes in order to take advantage of tax savings opportunities. In reality, this can mean the difference between success or failure.

A primary goal of any business should be to operate in such a way as to avoid (legally!) as many taxes as possible. Appropriate deductions may be taken for home maintenance and improvements, automobile expenses, telephone expenses, office and work space, and major purchases, as well as for items like safe deposit rental, stationery and business cards. As a business owner you can also take advantage of tax-deferred retirement plans and tax-deductible medical insurance.

This chapter is meant to give you a simplified understanding of tax law and practice. However, as stated before, it is imperative from the outset that you seek the counsel of an accountant who can guide you through specific tax issues and help you plan and implement strategies to minimize taxes.

Always bear in mind that being aware of how the tax system works, and paying only those taxes legally required, will be to your advantage. Knowing the facts about tax breaks will save you tax dollars, help you avoid unwise purchases, and guide you in better record keeping.

TYPES OF TAXES

Remember the old saying, "In this life you can be sure of only two things — death and taxes?" Well folks, you can run but you can't hide from the IRS.

All business owners must pay taxes to federal, state, and local governments. The following are the most common types of taxes.

FEDERAL TAXES

Federal taxes that apply to sole proprietors, partnerships, and S corporations, and their appropriate tax forms, are listed below. For **free** forms and publications, call your district IRS office or write to the government printing office. Also, numerous free forms and publications can be downloaded directly off the Internet.

IRS District Office
800-TAX-FORM

U. S. Government Printing Office
Superintendent of Documents
Washington, D.C. 20402

Or, particularly brave souls can call the IRS at the 800 number listed in the Government Pages of your telephone directory under "United States Government, IRS Forms."

- **1040** Individual Income Tax Return 1040C *Profit or Loss from Business or Profession*: This form is used to report the revenue, detailed deductible expenses, and resulting net income of your business.

- **1040ES** *Estimated Tax for Individuals*: This form is used to report quarterly best estimates of income tax you will owe for the calendar year, and to calculate amounts to pay quarterly.

- **1040SE** *Computation of Social Security Self-Employment Tax*: Your estimated tax payments will also include payment into your Social Security fund.

- **4562** *Depreciation and Amortization.*

If you have employees, you will also need to submit the following forms:

- **SS-4** With Circular E. This is the *Application for the Employer Identification Number (EIN)*: Circular E, the Employer's Tax Guide, explains the federal income and Social Security withholding requirements.

- **940** *Employer's Annual Federal Unemployment Tax Return*: This form is used to report and pay the Federal Unemployment Compensation Tax.

- **941** *Employer's Quarterly Federal Tax Return*: Use this form to report income tax withheld from employees' pay during the previous calendar quarter and Social Security tax that was withheld and matched by you, the employer.

- **W-2** *Employer's Wage and Tax Statement*: This form is used to report to the IRS and to your employees the taxes withheld and compensation paid to employees.

- **W-3** *Reconciliation/Transmittal of Income and Tax Statements*: This form is used to summarize information from the W-2 and is sent to the Social Security Administration.

- *Index to Tax Publications* (No. 048-004-01596-B)

- *Your Federal Income Tax* (Publication 17)

- *Tax Guide for Small Business* (Publication 334)

- *Starting a Business and Keeping Records* (Publication 583)

- *Business Reporting* (Publication 937)

- *Business Use of Your Car* (Publication 917)

- *Business Use of Your Home* (Publication 587)

- *Employer's Tax Guide* (Circular E)

- *Self-Employment Tax* (Publication 533)

- *Tax Information on Depreciation* (Publication 534)

- *Business Expenses* (Publication 535)

- *Retirement Plans for Self-Employed* (Publication 560)

- *Information on Excise Taxes* (Publication 510)

- *Tax Withholding and Estimated Tax* (Publication 510)

U. S. General Services Administration
Consumer Information Center
P.O. Box 100
Pueblo, CO 81002

- *Financial Management: How to Make a Go of Your Business* (Publication 130Y)

- *Starting and Managing a Business from Your Home* (Publication 132Y)

FORM 1099 AND YOUR BUSINESS'S INCOME TAXES

If you work as a noncorporate independent contractor for hospitals, clinics or physicians and are paid more than $600 in commissions, fees or other compensation including payments to outsourcers, you should receive a 1099 form in February or March of each year. Form 1099 is like the W-2 form that employees receive. Copies are sent to the IRS, to the state taxing agency, and to you.

If you are a sole proprietor, you must report your 1099 income on form 1040, Schedule C, *Profit or Loss From Business or Profession*. Your business expenses are also recorded on this form. You should consult a tax adviser and read the book *Smart Tax Write-offs* to make sure you are taking all business expenses you are entitled to. You will also have to attach 1040, Schedule SE — *Computation of Social Security Self-Employment Tax*.

TAX DEPOSITS

Independent contractors must deposit the three following taxes each quarter:

- federal income tax

- Social Security self-employment tax

- state income tax

The deposits must be carefully calculated or the IRS and state taxing agency (Franchise Tax Board in California) will assess fines. As a self-employed individual, you will have to pay estimated taxes quarterly.

189

If in doubt about how much to pay, you should pay at least as much as you paid the previous year, and in most cases the IRS cannot penalize you for underpayment of estimated tax. When your clients pay you, be sure to set aside money for taxes, including self-employment tax (in 1998, 15.3% of the first $68,400 of income and 2.9% of the excess). If you have any questions, it would be wise to talk to a tax consultant or call the IRS.

IRS
800-829-1040

The three taxes are paid with two forms: the federal 1040 ES (for federal income tax and Social Security self employment tax) and California's 540 ES (for state income tax). Tax deposits are due on April 15, June 15, September 15, and January 15.

> **NOTE**
>
> *To avoid income tax penalties, you must prepay 90% of the taxes owed for the current year or the equivalent of 100% of your tax liability of the previous year, or 110% if your previous year's adjusted gross income exceeded $150,000.*

Independent contractors pay taxes on their net income, which is gross income minus business expenses. An expense must be "reasonable and necessary" for it to be deductible. Exact deductions vary for each type of business and are continually changing. When estimating your business expense deductions it is wise to remember that the expenses must be "reasonable and necessary." Generally, the more you can prove something was used exclusively for your business, the easier it is to prove it is a legitimate deduction.

If you don't use equipment, car, or other items exclusively for business, you should keep records which clearly detail tax-deductible use: specific equipment used, dates of use, time, and purpose.

SOCIAL SECURITY TAXES (FICA)

All self-employed people must file a self-employment form when the annual profit claimed on Schedule C reaches $400. At this point, the self-employed person starts to pay into Social Security at a rate specified by the government. In 1998 the rate is 15.3% of the first $68,400 and 2.9% on any amount over $68,400.

Social Security benefits are available to the self-employed just as they are to wage earners. Your payment of self-employment tax contributes to your coverage under the Social Security system, which should eventually provide you with retirement benefits and medical insurance benefits (Medicare). To learn the amount in your account, contact the Bureau of Data Processing.

Bureau of Data Processing
Social Security Benefits
Baltimore, MD 21235

Paying this tax can be a shock, especially for those of us who worked as employees in the past. When working as an employee, the employee and employer each pay half of the Social Security tax. That advantage is lost, however, when a self-employed medical coder becomes solely responsible for payment of the entire tax.

The independent coder does get a break though since half the Social Security tax may be deducted from the self-employed's gross income.

CHECK YOUR SOCIAL SECURITY RECORD

The Social Security Administration (SSA) has thousands of uncredited earnings reports totaling hundreds of millions of dollars. If three years pass, the statute of limitations may prevent otherwise eligible recipients from correcting a mistake in their earnings records, and their Social Security benefits may be reduced as a result. Check your earnings record by filing SSA Form 7004 with your local SSA office. This is a free service and one which all independent coders should take advantage of, especially since we are paying **all** our FICA taxes.

EMPLOYER'S IDENTIFICATION NUMBER (EIN)

Partnerships, corporations, and sole proprietors that have employees are required to have an Employer's Identification Number (EIN). Sole proprietors without employees have the option of using their Social Security number or obtaining an EIN number.

The purpose of the EIN is to facilitate record keeping by the government. Failure to use the number on the appropriate form can result in a fine of $50 each time it is omitted.

An EIN is obtained by filing IRS Form SS-4, which is available from the IRS.

ESTIMATED TAX PAYMENTS — A HORROR STORY!

Taxes are withheld throughout the year from wages earned by employees. However, as a self-employed individual, you are responsible for making periodic payments of your estimated federal income tax.

A case in point: When one of the authors went into business, she was naive about tax law. At the end of her first year, she dutifully met with an accountant to discuss taxes. She was horrified when he informed her that she owed $14,000 in federal and state taxes on April 15th — all because she had not been making quarterly tax payments.

To avoid such a catastrophe, have your accountant set up a schedule of quarterly tax payments, which are due April 15th, June 15th, September 15th, and January 15th. These will include payment of federal income tax, Social Security tax or self-employment tax, and state income tax. This procedure will help you avoid a shock to your system and your checkbook when April 15th rolls around.

To avoid penalties in most cases, you must prepay at least 90% of the taxes owed for the current year or the equivalent of 100% of your tax liability of the previous year. You can request estimated tax payment forms from the IRS. As stated above, your accountant will also be able to give you the needed forms and advice, calculating the amount you owe each quarter.

STATE TAXES

Taxes vary from state to state, but most have an income tax. This tax is calculated on net income and is usually due at the same time you file federal tax returns. In some states, the tax is calculated on gross income, less certain qualified deductions.

Some states require employers to carry Workers' Compensation Insurance for all employees. Even though it is called insurance, it feels like a tax. The program can be managed by the state or by the insurance agent who carries your other business insurance. Contact your state administrators to research this issue.

HOME-SWEET-TAX-DEDUCTION

As a home-based business owner, you qualify for tax deductions for your home office — either as a portion of your rent or as depreciation. The amount of the allowable deduction is based on the percent of the home used for business purposes. For tax deduction purposes, the home-based office must meet the following criteria:

- Clearly separated from family living space

- Used exclusively for business purposes

- Used on a regular basis for business purposes

- Used as your principal place of business or used as a meeting place for you to interact with clients.

Keep in mind, however, that any business deduction taken for depreciation of your home office reduces the tax basis of your home and normally must be "recaptured" when you sell your home. "Recaptured" means you will pay income taxes at your regular rate instead of at the lower capital gains rate on that portion of your home sale profit represented by your home office depreciation.

There are two ways to calculate the percent of your home used for business purposes:

- One method is to divide the square feet in the home into the number of square feet used for business purposes. Thus, if in a 3000 square foot home, 1000 square feet of space is used for business, 33-1/3% of applicable home expenses can be claimed as a tax deduction.

• The other method for figuring space is to count the number of rooms (if they are nearly equal in size) and divide the number of rooms used for business purposes by the total number of rooms. If one room is used in a five-room house, then 1/5 or 20% of the home expenses are legitimate home-use business deductions.

Either method is acceptable, so use the one that results in the best benefit to you.

A percentage of the expenses listed below can be deducted from income as business expenses:

• Rent

• Mortgage interest

• Insurance premiums on home

• Utilities, including gas, electricity, and water

• Services such as trash and snow removal, house cleaning, and yard maintenance expenses

• Home repairs, including labor and supplies

Note that the TOTAL amount of the following expenses are also tax-deductible:

• Decorating, painting, and remodeling costs for the part of the home used solely for business purposes.

●Telephone — all long distance business calls and charges for extra business related services.

WHEN THE HOME OFFICE DEDUCTION IS NOT THE BEST OPTION

According to stringent IRS rulings, any home office that qualifies for the home-office deduction must be a distinct space that is specifically used for business. If you qualify for and take the deduction, when you subsequently sell your home, you may be forced to shell out income tax on the business portion of your gain instead of rolling all the profit into a reduction of the tax basis of your new home.

Here's how the IRS sees it: If a taxpayer claims a deduction for an in-home office, he or she has changed that portion of the property to a commercial tax status. So in the year the taxpayer sells the property, the business portion may not qualify for the much easier rules that allow rollover of the gain from the sale of the residential portion. Depending on your individual tax situation, you may want to plan ahead concerning the sale of your home and make sure it's considered a 100% residential property by claiming no home-office depreciation deductions. You should follow a similar strategy when planning to take the once-in-a-lifetime, post-age-55 exclusion of any capital gains taxes on the sale of your principal residence.

> ### NOTE
> *Tax laws change frequently. What holds true today may not necessarily be the case in future years. Consult your accountant about tax law changes that may affect your business.*

AUTOMOBILE EXPENSES

The legitimate business use of a car can generate significant tax deductions for small-business owners. Commuting is not deductible, but other business travel is: picking up and delivering work, client meetings, trips to the post office, trips to office supply stores, etc.

Keeping a mileage log in your car to document business use is still a smart idea. In addition to keeping a log book, keep the first and last repair bills of the year. If the car's mileage has been noted at the time of repair, you can present the bills to the IRS as proof of the number of miles you drove through the tax year.

The IRS offers two alternative methods for calculating the amount of automobile expenses:

1) **Standard mileage rate** method provides an umbrella deduction equal to the number of business miles you have driven during the year multiplied by 32.5 cents per mile. The standard mileage rate covers the cost of operating the car, including depreciation, maintenance and repairs, gasoline, oil, insurance and vehicle registration fees. Under this method, those expenditures are not separately deductible, but you can deduct tolls and parking fees in addition to the standard mileage rate calculation.

2) **Actual car expenses** method allows you to deduct the exact costs of each of the above items, as well as tires, garage rental fees, lease payment and even rental car costs. However, you can deduct only the percentage related to the business use of the car. For instance, if your records show that you drove 10,000 miles during the year but only 4000 miles

were business-related, you can deduct only 40% of actual car expenses.

The IRS lets you choose whichever method will lead to the higher deduction, so it is in your best interest to do both calculations. Remember, if you use a car primarily for business, the actual car expenses method may provide a significantly better deduction.

There are exceptions to the rules, most of which impact the deductibility of your car expenses, including lease payments and depreciation. The first "gotcha" is that if you use the standard mileage rate method the first time you report business use of your car to the Internal Revenue Service, you cannot subsequently depreciate that particular car using the accelerated depreciation method. However, if you calculate your first deduction using the actual expense method, you are allowed to toggle between the two methods in subsequent years.

Under the actual car expenses method, the total amount you can include for depreciation has IRS limitations. These are varying limits based on the year you start using your car for business and on the specific year of the depreciation.

Depreciation deductions apply only to cars you buy outright. If you lease a car, still more rules and exceptions apply. Lease payments are fully deductible if the car is used solely for business. If not, the deductible amount is in proportion to the percentage of miles driven for business. But Section 280F of the IRS code stipulates an add-back, an amount keyed to the value of the car, that you must declare as taxable income. The government's intent is to place a cap on the lease deduction that is equivalent to the ceiling on a depreciation deduction.

It is best to sit down with your accountant while you are shopping for that new car, not after you buy it. The two of you should calculate the tax deductions for both buying and leasing a car based on the assumed business use percentage including the add-back.

INTEREST ON CAR LOANS

You can deduct interest on the business use portion of a car loan. The nonbusiness use percentage is considered nondeductible interest on a personal loan.

WHO SHOULD LEASE AND WHO SHOULD BUY?

Consider leasing a car if you:

- like having a new car every 2-3 years
- want to drive a more expensive car and still have lower monthly payments
- like having the option of not making a down payment
- like having a car that's always in warranty in case something goes wrong
- hate having to sell or trade your old cars
- don't like tying up your money in depreciating assets

Consider buying a car if you:

- typically drive your cars for several years or until they fall apart
- drive more than 15,000 miles a year on average
- usually sell or trade your cars before they are fully paid for

- drive your cars hard or under rough conditions
- typically buy fad cars that quickly lose their resale value
- like to know you own your car

BUSINESS-RELATED TRAVEL EXPENSES

Whether you travel by air, rail, bus, or personal automobile, expenses associated with travel for business purposes are tax-deductible. Save your ticket stubs, credit card slips and checks to present as evidence of travel expenses.

EDUCATION EXPENSES

An added benefit of joining a professional association is that expenses incurred in attending meetings, including travel expenses, symposium or convention fees, and books can be tax-deductible.

Education expense is deductible if the education improves or maintains a skill required in your business. However, if the education is required to meet minimum education requirements of your present business, or if the education will qualify you for a new trade or business, the expense is not allowed.

Incidentally, any self-employed medical coding specialist can take a course in bookkeeping, computers or any other course that helps you run your business better and deduct the cost as a business expense.

> *"It is best to sit down with your accountant while you are shopping for that new car, not after you buy it."*

EXPENSING AND DEPRECIATION

Expensing means taking an income tax deduction for the entire cost of an item in the year it is purchased, up to a current limit of $18,500 per year. In 1999 it goes to $19,000, and in the year 2000, to $20,000. *Depreciation* is taking a deduction for business property ratably over its useful life of more than one year — usually at least five years.

Expensing is usually preferable to depreciation because a tax write-off (resulting in cash in your pocket instead of Uncle Sam's pocket) is more valuable earlier than later. However, under certain circumstances, depreciation may be preferable. Remember that the IRS does change depreciation rules periodically, so it might be wise to expense while you can. Again, check with your accountant and refer to IRS Publication 334 for small businesses.

RECORDS NEEDED FOR TAX PURPOSES

It is essential that you keep all receipts for business expenses and all miscellaneous receipts for out-of-pocket purchases, noting what was purchased on the back of the receipt. Use a simple accordion file — or any other system that works well for you — for storing all your receipts and checks for the year. Get in the habit of filing your receipts so you know where they are. This will help tremendously around tax time.

Your business checkbook will also be a valuable resource at tax time to calculate tax-deductible expenditures. The Internal Revenue Service can investigate a return for up to three years after it has been filed, so keep all records for at least three years. In fact, it wouldn't be a bad idea to keep your records for seven years or as long as you operate the business.

TAX SHELTERING THROUGH RETIREMENT PLANS

As your business grows and prospers, you should consider tax sheltering as a way to better protect your hard-earned money. A retirement plan tax shelter allows you to reduce taxes by investing a portion of your pretax income in special programs designed to defer payment of tax. Taxes are not avoided but simply postponed until you withdraw money from your fund at a later time, usually in retirement, when presumably you will be in a lower tax bracket.

Popular tax sheltering plans include the Simplified Employee Pension (SEP), Individual Retirement Account (IRA), and Qualified Profit Sharing Plans (Defined Benefit or Defined Contribution).

SIMPLIFIED EMPLOYEE PENSION (SEP)

A Simplified Employee Pension (SEP) is a retirement program whereby an employer makes contributions into employees' IRA accounts. For your one-person business, the pretax contribution is into your IRA. The SEP plan allows a higher contribution than an individual IRA and can be made to owner/employees over 70½ years old. The maximum contribution to a SEP is the lesser of 15% of employee compensation or $30,000. For the owner of a sole proprietorship the maximum contribution is limited to 13.043% of net Schedule C income less one half of self-employment tax percent.

SEPs are attractive for the following reasons:

- They are simple and easy to establish

- They can be established after the close of your business year and after April 15th

- They don't require IRS filing or Form 5500 reporting (which are required in profit sharing plans)

- There are no administration costs

- Contributions are tax deductible and elective (they do not have to be made every year)

- Contribution amount may vary from year to year, from zero to 15%

INDIVIDUAL RETIREMENT ACCOUNT (IRA)

The Individual Retirement Account (IRA) provides an excellent opportunity to establish a personal retirement program using pre-tax dollars. There are, however, two conditions that must be met to qualify for this plan: 1) You must not participate in any other type of retirement plan (other than Social Security), and 2) your adjusted gross income must be less than $40,000 in order to have deductibility.

If you meet the above criteria, the amount saved and earnings generated by an IRA are not currently taxable. The tax-free status continues until you retire. Even if you do not meet the above qualifications, you can put money into an IRA although the money deposited is not fully tax-deductible. However, the income earned on the account's investment is not taxed until withdrawal. The maximum amount you can contribute yearly to an IRA is presently $2000.

Although the IRA is not taxed until payments are received, after age 59½, IRA funds may be withdrawn without a 10% penalty should you become disabled. In the event of your death, the funds are paid to your beneficiary. As of 1998, you can also withdraw IRA funds without penalty in order to pay some medical expenses, for higher education, and for acquisition of a first home.

IRA plans are available through banks and savings and loans (certificates of deposit), money market and mutual funds, stockbroker-managed or self-directed IRA accounts, insurance companies annuity plans, and United States minted gold.

HEALTH INSURANCE

If you are a sole proprietor, partner in a partnership, or owner of an S corporation, you are allowed an income tax deduction of 45% of the cost of health insurance in 1998, 60% in 1999, 70% in 2002, and 100% in 2003. According to *Smart Tax Write-offs*, Rayve Productions, there is a way to make your personal health insurance premium 100% deductible. Your business can enroll your employee-spouse as an insured employee in your business's health insurance plan. The insurance premium for this employee is fully deductible, and you can then be covered in the plan as his or her spouse.

SHOULD YOU HIRE AN ACCOUNTANT, BOOKKEEPER OR TAX PREPARER?

Most of us have had experience balancing our own checkbooks and know some basic bookkeeping principles. However, business bookkeeping is much more detailed, and savvy professionals seek the best possible counsel affordable when establishing an accounting system. We recommend working with an accountant and/or a tax adviser. A knowledgeable bookkeeper may also be capable of setting up a basic system.

An accountant should be consulted a minimum of once or twice a year to analyze the books, prepare and analyze financial statements, and help with tax returns. The accountant can also advise you on financial decisions and help to chart the future course of your business based on an analysis of your financial records.

It is unfortunate, but true, that many businesses fail because of inadequate financial planning and visibility. It is crucial to set up and maintain a system that will be comfortable for you to maintain and use as a tool for running your business smartly.

Do your homework. Review a book such as *Easy Financials for Your Home-based Business* in order to get a basic understanding of your available choices. Then confer with a knowledgeable professional to help you set up your system. It is well worth your investment in time and money to set up a system that will give you the visibility to manage your business successfully. And these professional expenses are tax-deductible.

Beware of hiring a tax preparer instead of an accountant. This could cost you considerable money in the long run. Tax preparers may only be capable of working with the numbers you provide them and may not have the experience to pursue available tax breaks aggressively.

On other hand, an accountant who is knowledgeable about your type of business will be aware of tax advantages, suggesting desirable business actions. It is likely that the accountant will save you more money than his or her fees.

How do you select an accountant or a bookkeeper? Ask professional associates for recommendations. Carefully evaluate training, experience and references.

It is important to find an accountant or bookkeeper who has experience working with small businesses. To prevent any unpleasant surprises, be sure to discuss fees in advance with the bookkeeping or accounting service.

TECHNOLOGY UPDATES

*"Great software not only meets your business needs
but is also a pleasure to use."*

T he vendor "spin doctors" have always hyped the latest hardware
and software. Let's reflect on the trends we have seen in IS
(Information Systems) that were here . . . and then gone.

THE COMPUTERIZED PATIENT RECORD — HIGH TECH SYSTEMS THAT CAME AND WENT

In the '80s we saw **bedside computers** that were promoted as a way
to automate clinical care at its point of delivery. These systems never
quite made it to the mainstream because they were too narrowly focused
on nursing departments. Physicians document patient care everywhere
but at the patient bedside: their cars, homes, offices, nursing stations,
ER, medical records departments, etc.

> •**Smart Cards** were implemented to serve as a patient's link
> to the health care system, no matter where they were. The

smart card concept was a credit-card-type data system containing a tiny computer chip that allowed instant access to a patient's medical history by inserting the card in a reader-box. The problem with these cards was that they required regular updates. Every cardholder would have to be involved in this process and this was very difficult. If updated medical information was not available, it could result in inadequate patient care, patient injury or health care provider liability.

- **Computerized Patient Records (CPR)** have been promoted for years and now vendors will be promoting "workable" computerized record products. However, it is predicted that it will take still another decade to work out the bugs. In the future we may see a patient record that is less "chatty" and more streamlined. The CDR (clinical data repository) provides long-term storage for patient care information. The CDR objective is to provide caregivers with quick access to individual patient data and provide aggregate information for analyzing practice patterns.

In the 1998 Health Care Information Management Systems Society (HIMSS) Annual Leadership Survey (published in the June 1998 edition of *Advance, for Health Care Professionals*), 93% of the survey respondents (1380) took the survey and 79% indicated that United States health care facilities are making slow progress towards the computer based patient record (CPR). Respondents felt that full implementation is still a very distant goal in most organizations. Only 2% reported having a fully operational CPR system in place within their health care facility and 24% have not yet begun to plan for CPR implementation; 17% of respondents reported that they have developed a CPR implementation plan and another 17% have begun to install

CPR software and hardware. A smaller group, 10%, are currently evaluating the impact of the CPR system.

According to survey respondents, the system's greatest drawbacks include the following areas: 1) lack of standardized vocabulary, 23%; 2) inadequate information or IC infrastructure, 50%; 3) resistance of administrative staff, 14%.

Survey respondents also had concerns regarding security, with a breakdown of security issues as follows: 31% cited internal breaches of security as their number one concern; 21%, limits of existing security technology; and 16%, patients' lack of confidence in the security of medical records.

Thirty-one percent of the respondents reported that they plan to merge voice recognition technology into their organization, possibly within the next twelve months.

- **Picture Archiving and Communication Systems (PACs)**, were envisioned as dedicated networks for storing, managing and sending x-rays and other digital images like MRI, CT, ultrasound and nuclear medicine studies. These systems were very expensive, and doctors preferred old analog film, which they claimed was superior in sharpness to the digital images. These systems have been modified and are still in use.

- **Bar Codes** never really caught on in health care as they did in grocery stores. This concept was viewed by many as an unnecessary cost. Also, other technologies — computer touch screens and voice recognition systems as well as optical scanners — have elbowed bar codes to the sidelines. However, although not popularly accepted, many hospitals still use barcodes.

Many of these trendy ideas are now relics, made impractical by the growth of managed care, the shift from inpatient to outpatient care, and the emergence of integrated health systems. And, the personal computer revolution has made a major impact. Most of the costly mainframe systems have been replaced by inexpensive but powerful desktop computers.

THE FUTURE OF HEALTH CARE

"This time, like all times, is a very good one,
if we but know what to do with it."

—Ralph Waldo Emerson

S tudies have shown that health care facilities are continuing to restructure and downsize by consolidating services and eliminating many management and employee positions. Instead of the traditional inpatient setting, medical care is progressively moving toward outpatient services — outpatient surgery centers, urgent care centers, walk-in clinics, rural health centers, etc.

Interest in health care costs has increased dramatically. Although a national health care plan has not been successful to date, managed care and capitation are a reality. Today, instead of focusing on the individual patient as was done in the past, the focus of health care delivery and reimbursement is on the "community". Because the DRG system has been able to reduce medical costs for the Health Care Financing Administration (HCFA), other health care providers are utilizing similar reimbursement systems. Reimbursement is based on a "population" not an individual patient. Optimum reimbursement for services provided is dependent on the accuracy of the coded health care record.

As health care reform continues, the need for accurate coding will remain constant or grow. The true change will be in managed care, where the need for credentialed procedural coders will increase.

As a professional coder, the complete and thorough account of the diagnosis, procedures, complications comorbidities and signs/symptoms, and the proper DRG assignment is crucial for optimum reimbursement.

Accurate coding, which is the key to so much health care data, is absolutely essential within managed care because this system is data driven. Data is used in making all major decisions regarding patient care services, employees, and facility management. By analyzing data, the quality and cost-effectiveness of patient care and programs are evaluated, and based on these evaluations, short- and long-range goals are implemented. When negotiating capitated contracts, negotiators depend on statistical data to accurately portray the quality and cost-effectiveness of care. Such dependency on ever-increasing amounts of data will almost certainly result in increasing job opportunities for those who know how to readily produce the data required by this new system.

Coders must stay current and code to the highest level of specificity. As an independent coding contractor, keeping a sharp eye on health care reimbursement trends will be very important to your business success. Education about the DRG system is certainly going to be a number one priority for your background needs. Start now to gain the coding tools needed, and strengthen those coding skills which may be weak. You will need to know CPT and HCPCS Coding, so prepare for using these codes by taking the following action:

Evaluate your resources:

- •Coding Materials — Get the most recent CPT copy and update it annually.

- •Coding Expertise — Attend inservices or seminars on CPT coding.

- •Review Procedure Statements and Codes.

- •Training and Development — Never stop learning and growing. Keep up with new technology and trends that will give you a competitive edge.

- •Create a Master CPT and HCPCS Codes List.

FAVORITE REFERENCES AND RESOURCES

Advance — For Health Information Professionals
650 Park Avenue
Box 61556
King of Prussia, PA 19406-0956
610-265-7812
800-355-5627, ext. 149
610-265-8293
E-mail: HIMEDIT@merion.com

AHIMA (American Health Information Management Association)
515 North State Street
Chicago, Ill 60610
800-335-5535

> •**Time to Code** — This AHIMA coding reference catalog includes training and educational coding resources, reimbursement resources and general coding training resources.

American Medical Association (AMA), Celeste Kirschner
515 North State Street
Chicago, IL 60610
312-464-4733
312-464-4700, 4737, 5932
Fax 312-464-5849
800-621-8335

- ● **AMA-HCPCS Level II Code Book**

- ● **AMA-Color Coded ICD-9-CM Code Book**

- ● **AMA-CPT 1997 Professional Edition Code Book**

- ● **AMA-CPT Assistant** (resource for physician office coding)

California Health Information Association (CHIA)
5108 E. Clinton Way, Suite 113
Fresno, CA 93727-8509
209-251-5038
E-mail: CHIAPR1@aol.com
Voice 209-251-5038
Fax 209-251-5836

California Medical Review, Inc. (CMRI)
Citicorp Center, One Sansome Street, Suite 600
San Francisco, CA 94104-4448
415-677-2000
E-mail: http://www.cmri-ca.org/

CMRI is an independent, nonprofit, federally designated Quality Improvement Organization serving California's 3.8 million Medicare beneficiaries. CMRI has monitored healthcare quality for the state since 1984. A healthcare information company, CMRI works with consumers, providers, and purchasers to improve the quality of healthcare.

216

Channel Publishing, LTD
4750 Longley Lane, Suite 110
Reno, Nevada 89502
800-248-2882

- **The Educational Annotation of ICD-9-CM**

- **Faye Brown Coding Handbook**
  The Educational Annotation of ICD-9-CM

- **Clinotes "The Clinical Bridge from Disease to Coding"**

- **The Expanded ICD-9-CM** (Excellent!)
  Table of Drugs & Chemicals

Coding Clinic for ICD-9-CM
American Hospital Association (AHA)
One North Franklin
Chicago, Ill 60606
800-261-6246

Continuing Education (CE) credits available through the AHA.

The Coding Edge — Newsletter
Laguna Medical Systems
1401 N. El Camino Real, Suite 106
San Clemente, CA 92672
800-394-1040

Excellent monthly newsletter. You can submit coding questions.
CE credits available.

The Coding Registry
First Class Solutions, Inc.
2060 Concourse Drive
St. Louis, MO 63146
800-274-1214

CPT Coding Workbook
MedLearn (Medical Learning Incorporated)
245 East Sixth Street
St. Paul, MN 55101
800-252-1578
Fax 612-229-0835

For the Record — Newsletter
1288 Valley Forge Road, Suite 51
P.O. Box 2224
Valley Forge, PA 19482-2224
610-917-9300

J. A. Holloway & Associates, Inc.
P. O. Box 34003
Truckee, CA 96160
800-888-4966

> Educational workshops are also available through J. A. Holloway & Associates, Inc.

J. A. Thomas & Associates
Suite 111
1190 Winchester Parkway
Smyrna, Georgia 30080-82
770-438-8537

Medical Record Briefing
Opus Communications Fulfillment Center
P.O. Box 9214
Waltham, MA 02254-9214
800-650-6787

Medicode, Inc.
5225 Wiley Post Way, Suite 500
Salt Lake City, UT 84116-2889
800-999-4600
Fax 801-536-1011
http://www.medicode.com

- **The Surgical Cross-Coder**
  This cross-references all surgical CPT-4 codes. There are more than 100 illustrations to assist the coder in understanding complicated procedures and disease processes and more than 45 procedural illustrations that provide details of procedures such as arthroscopic knee, laminectomy, cystourethrotomy, etc. There are also anatomy and disease process illustrations to assist in locating the right code.

  Medicode, Inc. is a useful resource for up-to-date coding references and software. The company also has a Web site on the Internet where you can preview their products and publishes a newsletter, *Code Facts*, which you can receive twice a month, via fax if you like. This publication includes the latest coding and reimbursement news.

National Tumor Registrars Association, Inc.
505 E. Hawley Street
Mundelein, Illinois 60060
708-566-0833

St. Anthony's Publishing, Inc.
500 Montgomery Street, Suite 700
Alexandria, VA 22314-1561
800-632-0123

- St. Anthony's ICD-9-CM Code Book

- St. Anthony's DRG Optimizer

- St. Anthony's ICD-9-CM Code Book for Outpatient Services (Vol 1, 2 & 3)

- St. Anthony's HCPCS Level II Code Book

UNITED STATES CHAMBERS OF COMMERCE
(Courtesy of World Chamber of Commerce Directory, 970-663-3231)

● **ALABAMA** (Business Council of Ala.)
William F. O'Connor, Jr., President
2 N. Jackson; P.O. Box 76
Montgomery, 36101-0076
334-834-6000; fax 334-262-7371

● **ALASKA** (Alaska State C of C)
Pamela La Bolle, President
217 2nd St., #201
Juneau, 99801-1267
907-586-2323; fax 907-463-5515
asccjuno@ptialaska.net;
www.alaskachamber.com

● **AMERICAN SAMOA** (Chamber of
Commerce of American Samoa)
Salaia L. Gabbard, Mgr.
P.O. Box 2446,
Pago, Pago, 96799
phone & fax 684-699-6214
CHAMBER@samoatelco.com

● **ARIZONA** (Arizona C of C)
Tim Lawless, Pres./CEO,
Public Policy & Legislative Issues Only
1221 E. Osborn Rd., #100
Phoenix, 85014-5539
602-248-9172; fax 602-265-1262
info@azchamber.com;
www.azchamber.com

● **ARKANSAS** (Arkansas C of C)
Ron Russell, Executive Vice President
410 S. Cross; P.O. Box 3645
Little Rock, 72203-3645
501-374-9225; fax 501-372-2722
rrussell@ascc-aia.org;
statechamber-aia.dina.org

● **CALIFORNIA** (California State C of C)
Allan Zaremberg, President
1201 K St., 12th Floor; P.O. Box 1736
Sacramento, 95812-1736
916-444-6670; fax 916-444-6685
www.calchamber.com

● **COLORADO** (Colorado Assn. of
Comm. & Ind.)
Sam Cassidy, Pres./CEO
1776 Lincoln St., #1200
Denver, 80203-1029
303-831-7411; fax 303-860-1439
caci@coloradobusiness.com;
www.businesscolorado.com

● **CONNECTICUT** (Conn. Bus. & Ind. Assn.)
Kenneth O. Decko, President
370 Asylum St.
Hartford, 06103-2022
860-244-1900; fax 860-278-8562
www.cbia.com

- **DELAWARE** (Delaware State C of C)
John M. Burris, President
1201 N. Orange St., #200; P.O. Box 671
Wilmington, 19899-0671
302-655-7221; fax 302-654-0691

- **DISTRICT OF COLOMBIA**
(Dist. of Columbia C of C)
Kwasi Holman, Exec. V.P.
1301 Pennsylvania Ave. N.W., #309,
20004
202-347-7201; fax 202-347-3537

- **FLORIDA** (Florida C of C)
Frank M. Ryll, Jr., President
136 S. Bronough St.; P.O. Box 11309
Tallahassee, 32302-3309
850-425-1200; fax 850-425-1260
fccpolicy@supernet.net;
www.flchamb.com

- **GEORGIA** (Georgia C of C)
Lindsay Thomas, President
233 Peachtree St., #200
Atlanta, 30303-1504
404-223-2264; fax 404-223-2290

- **GUAM** (Guam C of C)
Eloise R. Baza, President
173 Aspinall Ave., #101; P.O. Box 283
Agana, 96932
011-671-472-6311; 671-472-8011;
fax 011-671-472-6202
gchamber@guamchamber.com.gu;
www.guamchamber.com.gu

- **HAWAII** (C of C of Hawaii)
Stanley Hong, President
1132 Bishop St., #200
Honolulu, 96813-2830
808-545-4300; fax 808-545-4309

- **IDAHO** (No State Chapter)

- **ILLINOIS** (Illinois State C of C)
Dennis Whetstone, Pres./CEO
311 S. Wacker Dr., #1500
Chicago, 60606-6619
312-983-7100; fax 312-983-7101

- **INDIANA** (Indiana C of C)
Christopher Lamothe, Pres./CEO
115 W. Washington St., #850S,
Indianapolis, 46204-3407
317-264-3110; fax 317-264-6855
cplm@indy.net
www.indianachamber.com

- **IOWA** (Iowa Dept. of Eco. Dev.)
David Lyons, Director
200 E. Grand
Des Moines, 50309
515-242-4700; fax 515-242-4759

- **KANSAS** (Kansas C of C & Ind.)
John D. Fowler, Pres./CEO
835 S.W. Topeka Blvd.
Topeka, 66612-1671
785-357-6321; fax 785-357-4732

- **KENTUCKY** (Kentucky C of C)
Ken Oilschlager, President
464 Chenault Rd.; P.O. Box 817
Frankfort, 40602-0817
502-695-4700; fax 502-695-6824

- **LOUISIANA** (Louisiana Assn. of
Business & Industry)
Daniel Juneau, President
3113 Valley Creek Dr., P.O. Box 80258
Baton Rouge, 70898-0258
504-928-5388; fax 504-929-6054

- **MAINE** (Maine C of C & Business
Alliance)
Dana F. Connors, President
7 Community Drive
Augusta, 04330-9412
207-623-4568; fax 207-622-7723
staff@mainechamber.org;
www.mainechamber.org

222

- **MARYLAND** (Maryland C of C)
  Champe C. McCulloch, President
  60 West St., #100
  Annapolis, 21401-2479
  410-269-0642; 301-261-2858;
  fax 410-269-5247;
  mcc@mdchamber.org;
  www.mdchamber.org

- **MASSACHUSETTS**
  (Massachusetts C of C)
  Richard Piazza, President
  34 Market St.
  Everett, 02149
  617-389-4900; fax 617-387-0051
  majsccl@aol.com

- **MICHIGAN** (Michigan C of C)
  James Barrett, President
  600 S. Walnut St.
  Lansing, 48933-2200
  517-371-2100; fax 517-371-7224

- **MINNESOTA** (Minnesota State C of C)
  David Olson, President
  30 E. 7th St., #1700
  Saint Paul, 55101
  612-292-4650; 800-821-2230;
  fax 612-292-4656

- **MISSISSIPPI** (Mississippi Econ. Council)
  Blake Wilson, President
  P.O. Box 23276
  Jackson, 39225-3276
  601-969-0022; fax 601-353-0247

- **MISSOURI** (Missouri C of C)
  Mr. Jo Frappier, President
  428 E. Capitol Ave.; P.O. Box 149
  Jefferson City, 65102
  573-634-3511; fax 573-634-8855
  mchamber@computerland.net;
  www.computerland.net/ ~ mchamber

- **MONTANA** (Montana C of C)
  David Owen, President
  2030 11th Ave., P.O. Box 1730
  Helena, 59601
  406-442-2405; fax 406-442-2409

- **NEBRASKA** (Nebraska C of C & Ind.)
  Jack Swartz, CCE, CAE, President
  P.O. Box 95128
  Lincoln, 68509-5128
  402-474-4422; fax 402-474-5681
  ncchamber@sescor.com

- **NEVADA** (Nevada State C of C)
  David Howard, Legislative Affairs
  Director
  P.O. Box 3499
  Reno, 89505
  702-686-3030; fax 702-686-3038

- **NEW HAMPSHIRE** (Business and
  Industry Assn. of New Hampshire)
  John D. Crosier, President
  122 N. Main
  Concord, 03301
  603-224-5388; fax 603-224-2872

- **NEW JERSEY** (New Jersey C of C)
  Joan Verplanck, President
  216 W. State St.
  Trenton, 08608
  609-989-7888; fax 609-989-9696

- **NEW MEXICO** (Assn. of Commerce
  & Industry of New Mexico)
  John A. Carey, President
  P.O. Box 9706
  Albuquerque, 87119-9706
  505-842-0644; fax 505-842-0734
  aci@tcchnet.nm.org;
  www.technet.nm.org/aci

- **NEW YORK** (No State Chapter)

- **NORTH CAROLINA** (North Carolina Citizens for Business & Industry)
  Phillip J. Kirk, Jr., President
  225 Hillsborough St., #460;
  P.O. Box 2508
  Raleigh, 27602-2508
  919-836-1400; fax 919-836-1425

- **NORTH DAKOTA** (Greater North Dakota Assn.)
  Dale O. Anderson, President
  2000 Schafer St.; P.O. Box 2639
  Bismarck, 58502
  701-222-0929; fax 701-222-1611
  gnda@btigate.com

- **OHIO** (Ohio C of C)
  Andrew E. Doehrel, President
  P.O. Box 15159
  Columbus, 43215-0159
  614-228-4201; fax 614-228-6403

- **OKLAHOMA** (State of Oklahoma Assn.of Business & Industry)
  Richard P. Rush, CCE, Pres./CEO
  330 N.E. 10th St.
  Oklahoma City, 73104-3200
  405-235-3669; fax 405-235-3670

- **OREGON** (No State Chapter)

- **PENNSYLVANIA** (Pennsylvania Chamber of Business and Industry)
  Floyd W. Warner, President
  One Commerce Square; 417 Walnut St.
  Harrisburg, 17101-1902
  717-255-3252; 800-225-7224;
  fax 717-255-3298
  www.pachamber.org

- **PUERTO RICO** (Puerto Rico C of C)
  Edgardo Bigas, Exec. Vice President
  P.O. Box 9024033
  San Juan, 00902-4033
  787-721-6060; fax 787-723-1891

- **RHODE ISLAND** (No State Chapter)

- **SOUTH CAROLINA** (South Carolina State C of C)
  S. Hunter Howard J., Pres./CEO
  1201 Main St., #1810
  Columbia, 29201-3254
  803-799-4601; fax 803-779-6043
  nikkim@sccc.org; www.sccc.org

- **SOUTH DAKOTA** (South Dakota Chamber of Commerce & Industry)
  Ray Trankle, President
  P.O. Box 190
  Pierre, 57501-0190
  605-224-6161; 800-742-8112;
  fax 605-224-7198

- **TENNESSEE** (No State Chamber)

- **TEXAS** (Texas Assn. of Business & Chambers of Commerce)
  Dane Harris, President
  1209 Nueces; P.O. Box 2989
  Austin, 78768
  512-477-6721; fax 512-477-0836
  hdharris@tabcc.org; www.tabcc.org

- **UTAH** (Utah State C of C)
  Jack Howard, President
  P.O. Box 6022
  Salt Lake City, 84106
  435-882-0690; fax435-833-0946
  chamber@trilobyte.net

- **VERMONT** (Vermont State C of C)
  Christopher G. Barbieri, President
  P.O. Box 37
  Montpelier, 05601-0037
  802-223-3443; fax 802-223-4557
  vtchambr@together.net;
  www.vtchamber.com

- **VIRGIN ISLANDS** (St. Thomas-St. John C of C)
  Joe S. Aubain, Exec. Director
  6-7 Dronningens Gade, P.O. Box 324
  St. Croix, 00851-4369
  340-776-0100; fax 340-776-0588
  chamber@usvi.net

- **VIRGINIA** (Virginia C of C)
  Hugh D. Keogh, President
  9 S. Fifth St.
  Richmo

GLOSSARY

A

AAPC: American Academy of Procedural Coders — Professional network of CPT Coders.

Abuse: An incident or practice of a provider, physician, etc. which is inconsistent with accepted and sound medical, business, or fiscal practices and could be considered fraudulent. The incident or practice could also directly or indirectly results in unnecessary costs or improper reimbursements for services that fail to meet professionally recognized standards of care or are medically unnecessary.

Accredited: Status of health care organizations that meet the standards of national accrediting organizations, Joint Commission on Accreditation of Healthcare Organizations (JCAHO) and the National committee for Quality Assurance (NCQA).

Accredited Records Technician (ART): A person who has completed a course of instruction, passed an examination, and accomplished entry-level certification in medical records management from the American Health Information Management Association (AHIMA).

Admission: The process of registering a patient for service. In a hospital, admission usually involves an overnight stay. In an ambulatory care facility, length of stay is usually one day.

ALOS: Average Length of Stay.

AHA: American Hospital Association

AHIMA: American Health Information Management Association.

Allowed Amount: The amount determined by Medicare to be the maximum amount allowable for any given service.

AMA: American Medical Association. *Also,* Against Medical Advice

Ambulatory Care: A variety of health services that are provided on an outpatient basis, in contrast to services provided in the home or to inpatients. Many inpatients may be ambulatory, but the term ambulatory care usually refers to patients who travel to locations other than their home to receive services and then leave the same day.

Ambulatory Surgical Center (ASC): A facility that operates exclusively for the purpose of providing outpatient surgical services.

AMLOS (Arithmetic Mean Length of Stay): Average number of days patients within a given DRG stay in the hospital, also referred to as the average length of stay.

Ancillary Services: Inpatient services other than basic room and board and professional services, and hospital outpatient services other than professional services. They include services such as radiology, drug, laboratory, emergency room and home health.

Attending Physician: The physician providing the major portion of care or having primary responsibility for the care of the patient's major condition or diagnosis.

Authentication (of an entry in a medical record): The process of confirming the content of a health care entry by such means as written signature, identifiable entry, biometric identifier, or computer key. In practice, authentication usually involves countersigning a verbal or telephone order or signing the typed copy of a dictated document to confirm it was accurately transcribed.

Authorship (of an entry in a medical record): The process of identifying a health care practitioner who has released a health care entry for use, by writing, dictation, keyboard, or keyless data entry. In practice, authorship usually involves signing — or using some other method besides signing — to indicate authorship and authenticity of a dictated report.

B

Billed Amount: The amount charged for each service performed by the provider.

C

Capitation: A provider receives a fixed payment per member, per month, for which the provider must perform specific services. Though capitation involves less administrative cost than other payment methods, providers must assume the risk that the fixed payment will cover the costs of patient care needs.

Case Management: A process through which a single health care professional has the responsibility for monitoring the allocation and coordination of a patient's overall care to maximize effectiveness, reduce unnecessary procedures and minimize patient discomfort.

Case Mix: The diagnosis-specific makeup of a hospital's work load, which directly influences the lengths of stay and the intensity, cost, and scope of services provided by the hospital.

CC: **C**omplication *or* **C**omorbid **C**ondition of patient.

CCS: **C**ertified **C**oding **S**pecialist.

CCS-P: **C**ertified **C**oding **S**pecialist — **P**hysician-Base

Clinic: A facility or portion thereof used for diagnosis and treatment of outpatients. Also may be loosely defined to include physicians' offices.

CMI (**C**ase-**M**ix **I**ndex): The sum of all DRG relative weights, divided by the overall number of Medicare cases.

Concurrent Review: Case review conducted while a patient is in treatment, as opposed to retrospective review, which occurs after treatment and, therefore, cannot affect treatment.

Continuation: In the insurance context, when a covered person who would otherwise lose insurance coverage due to termination of employment, divorce, etc., is allowed to "continue" his or her coverage under conditions specified in the plan, as opposed to under any law. Providers must be aware of "continuation" limits.

Correct Coding Initiative (CCI): The national rebundling initiative that ensures comprehensive, component, and mutually exclusive procedures are not inappropriately paid.

Covered Services: Services rendered to patients that are reimbursable by the program to the provider.

Comparative Performance Report (CPR): A report that profiles physicians' billing patterns within an area. The report provides comparative data regarding utilization patterns for physicians in the same specialty/location.

CPR: Computerized Patient Record

Current Procedural Terminology (CPT): Numeric procedures codes that are Level II of the HCPCS coding system.

CQI: Continuous quality improvement.

Credentialing: The two-pronged process that involves establishing requirements and evaluating individual qualifications for entry into a particular status, such as medical staff membership. First, credentialing considers and establishes the professional training, experience and other requirements for medical staff membership. Second, credentialing involves obtaining and evaluating evidence of the qualifications of individual applicants. Most frequently, credentialing applies to medical staff membership; however, it also applies to the process hospital personnel departments use to evaluate applicants for other positions.

D

Date of Service: The date when a service was actually provided.

Denial: A determination that certain care or services cannot be reimbursed.

Department: In a hospital, a major unit of the medical staff, headed by a chair, director or chief, usually devoted to providing clinical service in one specialty area.

Departmental QA (or Departmental QA/I): The quality-related activities that, before 1994, the JCAHO required to be carried out by each major medical staff department. This is no longer a JCAHO requirement.

Department of Health and Human Services (DHHS): The federal department that oversees Medicare and Medicaid programs.

Diagnosis: The condition, cause of illness, or disease of the patient.

Diagnostic Related Group (DRG): A classification system developed at Yale University using 400 major diagnostic categories (based on the ICD-9 codes) that assigns patients into case types. Designed to facilitate the utilization review process, DRGs are also used to analyze the patient case-mix in hospitals and determine their reimbursement policies.

Direct Contracting: Individual or groups of employers contract directly with providers for health care services with no managed care intermediary (i.e., HMO, PPO, EPO) to customize services for employees.

Discharge Days: For each patient, the total number of inpatient days between admission and discharge dates. In calculating total inpatient days, the day of admission is included in the count, but not the day of discharge.

DOS: Date of Service.

E

E-Codes: Supplementary classification of ICD-9-CM, containing "External Causes of Injury and Poisoning". This section of codes is provided to permit the classification of environmental events, circumstances, and conditions as the cause of injury, poisoning and other adverse effects.

Ethics: A system or set of moral standards, values or principles; essential quality; the rules of conduct adopted by a given group or profession and to which members are expected to conform.

A system or set of moral principles recognized within a given group or profession.

F

Facility: The buildings, including the physical plant, equipment and supplies used in providing health care services. The major types of health care facilities include hospitals and nursing homes.

FAX: Facsimile machine/copy.

FCA: Federal False Claims Act

Fee-for-Service (FFS): A traditional payment system in which the physician or hospital bills the patient or insurer for each visit and service provided.

Fee Schedule: A list of certain services and payable amounts indicating the maximum payment for the service.

Fraud: The intentional deception or misrepresentation by an individual or entity, knowing it to be false and that the deception could result in some unauthorized self benefit.

Freestanding: Not part of a hospital (neither structurally connected to nor organizationally considered part of a hospital); not hospital-based.

G

Grouper: A software program that assigns DRGs.

H

Hardware: The physical components of a computer system, such as a computer, monitor, disk drive, and printer.

Health Care Financing Administration (HCFA): A division of the Department of Health and Human Services that administers Medicare and certain aspects of Medicaid. HCFA is responsible for determining which facilities meet federal quality standards for providing health care to beneficiaries.

HCPCS: Hospital Common Procedural Coding System.

HMO (Health Maintenance Organization): A legal entity or organized health care system that provides directly or arranges for a comprehensive range of basic and supplemental health care services to a voluntarily enrolled population in a geographic area on a primarily prepaid and fixed periodic basis. This term is defined by federal law in the Health Maintenance Organization Act of 1973 (Public Law 93-222).

Home Health Services: Home medical services.

Hospice: A facility that cares for terminally ill patients, with more emphasis on meeting the psychosocial needs of patients and/or families.

Hospital: Generally, an institution with an organized medical staff whose primary function is to provide diagnostic and therapeutic inpatient services for a variety of medical conditions, both surgical and nonsurgical.

I

ICD-9-CM: International Classification of Diseases. Modification developed in the United States based on the official version of the World Health Organization's International Classification of Diseases, 9th Revision, and designed for classification of morbidity and mortality information for statistical reporting purposes and information retrieval.

Indemnification: A negotiated contract provision under which one party to the contract agrees to pay any judgments, costs and attorney fees incurred by the other for acts or omissions that are the fault of the first. It is important for providers to insist on a "mutual" indemnification provision in any contract with a managed care entity.

Indicator (or clinical indicator): A quantitative measure of a clinically important process or outcome of care, usually expressed as a rate.

J

JCAHO: **J**oint **C**ommission on **A**ccreditation of **H**ealthcare **O**rganizations.

K-L

Length of Stay (LOS): The duration of an inpatient's stay in a hospital, which is calculated by subtracting the admit date from the discharge date. A patient admitted and discharged on the same day has a calculated length of stay of one day.

LTC (Long Term Care): Skilled nursing/intermediate care (non-acute).

M

Malpractice: Legal liability against a physician or a health care organization resulting from negligent or unprofessional treatment in the practice of a health care professional.

Managed care: A health care plan, such as an HMO style plan, that attempts to monitor and control the quality, cost effectiveness, and resource utilization of doctors, hospitals, and other health care facilities as they provide service to patients. Also, the organization of various types of health care providers into administrative networks in which they collaborate, refer patients to each other and share funding.

Maximize: Raise to highest degree possible.

Medi-Cal (Medicaid): A medical coverage program, jointly funded by state and federal governments, for those residents who qualify because their annual income falls below the state or nationally indicated poverty level.

Medical Review: The review of medical records or information as it relates to services rendered and billed by a provider or beneficiary for payment. This review is performed by medical staff physicians, registered nurses, or other appropriate medical personnel.

Medical Staff: The semiautonomous group of physicians, other licensed independent practitioners, and other such health care professionals permitted by state law and a hospital to take responsibility as a group for specified aspects of hospital operation. The medical staff is one of the three key parts of hospital governance. (The other two key parts of hospital governance are the governing board and the hospital administration.)

Medicare: A federal health insurance program that provides coverage for people sixty-five and older, for certain disabled people, and for some people with end-stage renal disease (ESRD). Medicare was enacted into law in 1965 by Congress through Title XVIII of the Federal Social Security Act and is managed by the Health Care Financing Administration (HCFA), a branch of the Department of Health and Human Services (DHHS).

Minimize: Reduce to the least possible degree or amount.

Modifiers: Two-digit codes that indicate services or procedures have been altered by some specific circumstance. Modifiers do not change the definition of the reported procedure codes.

N

NCQA: National Committee on Quality Assurance.

Netizens: Internet Citizens.

Noncovered Services: Services not covered by Medicare or other healthcare plans and which the patient is responsible to pay.

Nosology: 1) The branch of medicine dealing with the systematic classification of diseases. 2) A list or classification of diseases.

Nursing Home: Generally speaking, a residence facility that primarily provides custodial care such as help in eating, bathing, taking medicine, and toileting. Medicare does not cover custodial care if that is the only care needed. It is important to remember that not all nursing homes are skilled nursing facilities (SNF).

O

Omnibus Budget Reconciliation Act of 1990 (OBRA): A legislative act passed by Congress that provided for replacing the then-current reasonable charge mechanism of actual, customary, and prevailing charges with a Resource Based Relative Value Scale Fee Schedule beginning in 1992, with the transition period lasting until 1996.

Optimize: Make the most of; develop or realize to the utmost extent; obtain the most efficient or optimum use of. DRG optimization helps increase Medicare DRG payments and case-mix index, improve coding quality, reduce PRO risks and improve physician documentation.

Ordering Physician: The physician who orders a service or diagnostic test.

OSHPD: Office of Statewide Health Planning and Development.

Outpatient: A person who receives medical, dental, or other health-related services in a hospital or other health care institution but who is not lodged there.

P

Participating: An eligible provider who has entered into an agreement to accept assignment for services rendered.

Payers: People or businesses that have purchased coverage and/or paid for health care services (government, employers, and insurers).

Patient Eligibility: Requirements entitling individuals to benefits.

Patient Mix: The different types of patients served in a hospital in terms of such characteristics as age, sex, diagnosis, and residence.

Peer Review: Evaluation of a physician's performance by other physicians usually within the same geographic area and medical specialty.

Per Case: A method of payment in which a provider receives a payment determined by case-mix for a particular patient.

Policies and Procedures: Detailed technical directives and guidance that are outlined in documents. Often, policies are statements of purpose or objectives and procedures are statements of how purposes or objectives will be attained. They usually appear in the same document.

PPO (**P**referred **P**rovider **O**rganization): A health care organization formed by a hospital or physician group to contract with an insurer for health care provided to a defined population. PPOs are not exclusive providers of care to insured groups, but they usually offer lower charges to the insured groups in return for their influence in channeling patients to providers participating in the PPO. (Also see Preferred Provider Organization below.)

Practice Guidelines: Statements, either narrative or pictorial, describing recommended approaches to diagnosis or treatment of specified diseases, injuries, or conditions.

Preferred Provider Organization (PPO): A system designed to be an alternative to HMOs. Health care providers define a population to service at an agreed-upon fee schedule. (Also see PPO above.)

PRO (Peer Review Organization): Peer review organization; an organization that reviews appropriateness and quality of care for beneficiaries of the Medicare program.

Procedure Code: A CPT or HCPCS code used by a physician or provider of services to describe the procedure or service rendered to the patient.

Profiling: Collection and analysis of an individual practitioner's practice statistics for evaluation purposes.

Prospective Reimbursement: Any method of paying health care providers according to rates established in advance.

Provider: A person or organization that provides health care services (e.g., physician, hospital, home health agency).

Q

Quality Assessment/Improvement (QA/I): The term adopted by the JCAHO in 1993 to describe the activities required of hospitals to monitor and maintain the quality of patient care.

Quality of Care: Evaluation of the performance of medical providers according to the degree to which the process of care increases the probability of outcomes desired by patients.

R

RBRVS: Resource Based Relative Value Scale (see below).

Referring Physician: The physician who refers a patient for service or supply.

Registered Record Administrator (RRA): The recognition awarded by the AHIMA to individuals who possess the required credentials and pass the required examination that demonstrate competence in the management of health information record departments.

Rejected Claim: A returned claim that is not processed because the service is not covered or essential information may be missing.

Reimbursement: Repayment of money spent; compensation for expenses.

Resource Based Relative Value Scale (RBRVS): A scale that assigns values to procedures. Used to establish the Medicare Fee Schedule.

Retrospective Review: The determination of medical necessity, coverage, or payment for services that have already been rendered.

Review: A formal level of appeal following the initial processing of a claim. This may require additional documentation for review to support the initial claim for services.

Risk Management: An administrative activity aimed to prevent the loss of hospital resources resulting from actual or alleged accidents, neglect, or incompetence.

ROM (Read Only Memory): Programs or instructions that are permanently stored or "hard wired" in a computer.

Rural Health Clinics: Clinics that provide various medical services to patients in sparsely populated areas.

S

Severity of Illness (SOI): A method of categorizing and describing privileges by seriousness and hazardousness of the illness and conditions for which the privileges are offered.

SNF (Skilled Nursing Facility): A specialized health care facility or a distinct part of a hospital which provides skilled nursing care and supportive care to patients whose primary need is for skilled nursing care on an extended basis. The SNF provides 24-hour patient care and, as a minimum, includes medical, nursing, dietary and pharmaceutical services, as well as a variety of activity programs.

SNODO (**S**tandard **N**omenclature **o**f **D**iseases and **O**perations): An older nomenclature system in which each disease is classified to both anatomical location and etiology.

Social Security Administration: The branch of the Department of Health and Human Services that operates the various programs funded under the Social Security Act. It also determines when an individual becomes eligible for Medicare benefits.

Standard of Care: A legal standard defined as the level of care provided by the majority of physicians in a particular clinical situation.

Swing Beds: Hospital-based acute care beds that may be used alternatively to serve as long term care beds.

T

The Joint: Commonly used, informal term for the Joint Commission on Accreditation of Healthcare Organizations.

U

UHDDS (**U**niform **H**ospital **D**ischarge **D**ata **S**et): The hospital discharge data set periodically issued by the U.S. Department of Health and Human Services.

Utilization Review (UR): The examination and evaluation of the efficiency and appropriateness of all health care services.

V-Z

V-Codes (VO1-V82): Supplementary Classification of ICD-9-CM, containing "Factors Influencing Health States" and "Contact with Health Services". This classification is provided to deal with occasions when circumstances other than a disease or injury classifiable to categories 001-999 (the main part of ICD) are recorded as "diagnoses" or "problems".

APPENDIX

EXHIBIT

EXHIBIT I

The Official Position of

AMERICAN HEALTH INFORMATION®
MANAGEMENT ASSOCIATION

Medical Transcription
Industry Alliance

The **American Health Information Management Association (AHIMA)** is a national association of more than 37,000 medical record and health information management (HIM) professionals. AHIMA members work throughout the healthcare industry in settings ranging from physicians' offices and hospitals to ambulatory care facilities, long term care facilities, and managed care organizations. The **Medical Transcription Industry Alliance (MTIA)** is a nonprofit membership association of medical transcription companies. It aims to promote the education of individuals and corporations with respect to, and to promote the development of, applications of voice information management and telecommunications technology to the healthcare industry.

Issue: Confidential Health Information and the Internet

Background

The Internet, a network of several million computers, serves as a global information highway. Applications available on the Internet include electronic mail, online conversations and discussion lists, information retrieval, and bulletin boards. As the healthcare industry increasingly adopts information technology, several new uses of the Internet involving confidential health information are being developed and implemented.

Caregivers and patients use electronic mail to communicate. Patient databases are stored on the Internet, with some providers storing complete patient records in Internet-accessible sites. Physicians and other caregivers may use the Internet to discuss unusual cases and obtain advice from others with expertise in treating a particular disease or condition. Patients, too, use the Internet to seek information about their illnesses.

In the health information arena, text and voice files are being transmitted via the Internet. In a typical scenario, a healthcare provider dictates a report, which is stored in a digital format and transmitted via the Internet to a transcription setting. The voice file is stored temporarily on a hard drive until transcription is complete. The completed text is then transmitted back via the Internet to a data repository. Admission, discharge, and transfer (ADT) files (including patient names, dates of admission and discharge, and attending physician names) are also transmitted via the Internet to transcription services and individual transcriptionists. Electronic mail is used for communication between supervisors and employees working both on- and off-site. At times, when a transcriptionist needs help completing a report, pertinent sections from a patient's record may be quoted to provide context for filling in missing information.

Security Concerns

The Internet is not secure, and confidential information transmitted via the Internet may be intercepted and read by unauthorized persons. Commonly used Internet protocols may allow information to be altered or deleted without this being evident to either the sender or receiver.

Patients may be unaware that their personally identifiable health information is being maintained or transmitted via the Internet, and they may be subject to discrimination, embarrassment, or other harm if this confidential information is accessed by unauthorized individuals.

Recommendations

Health information applications on the Internet have the potential to bring great benefit to patient care but may also result in significant harm if they are improperly designed, monitored, or used. To protect the confidentiality and integrity of patient health information, the American Health Information Management Association (AHIMA) and the Medical Transcription Industry Alliance (MTIA) make the following recommendations:

- Applications on the Internet that contain patient-identifiable health information must be carefully designed to protect the confidentiality of the information.

- Appropriate security measures and available technologies should be employed to protect confidential health information from unauthorized access or alteration. These measures include encryption, secure transmission protocols, and firewalls.

- Text, voice, image and other patient files transmitted or maintained on the Internet should be encrypted to protect their confidentiality. Whenever possible, patient-identifiable information should exist as a separate file rather than part of the transcribed text document.

- Photographs or other images that may identify a patient should be used in Internet applications only with the express written consent of the patient or his/her legal representative.

- When a transcriptionist completes a document, it should be transmitted back to the transcription service bureau with no files (text, voice, or image) remaining on the hard drive of the transcriptionist's computer. Temporary files containing patient-identifiable information should be deleted as soon as they are no longer needed. Files such as patient admission lists should be deleted automatically or returned to the originator when the transcriptionist logs off at the close of each business day. Any files stored outside the transcription service bureau should have the same level of physical and electronic security as files kept by the service bureau.

- Print functions should be limited. Off-site transcriptionists should not be allowed to print copies of reports.

- Audit trails should record all individuals who access, modify, or delete any report.

- If patients and caregivers will use electronic mail to communicate, such communications should be limited to non-confidential information. If confidential information will be transmitted via electronic mail, that information should be encrypted to protect its confidentiality.

- If caregivers use electronic mail, bulletin boards, or online discussion groups to discuss a patient's case, no patient-identifiable information should be included. If electronic mail is used to discuss a case, that transmission should be encrypted.

- Client-side file caching by an Internet browser should be disabled. This prevents the localized save of patient data on the client machine.

- Transcription service bureaus should educate their employees and contractors about privacy and confidentiality issues, including use of electronic mail and online discussions ("chat rooms"). Written confidentiality agreements addressing these issues should be signed by each employee or contractor at the time of hire. Written acknowledgement should be signed on an annual basis thereafter to remind individuals of their ongoing responsibility for protecting the confidentiality of health information. Such agreements should be updated periodically to address issues raised by the use of new technologies.

- Organizations should develop, implement, and enforce policies and procedures to protect confidential information in Internet applications.

Summary

The use of new information technologies to support healthcare should not be discouraged, but they need to be carefully designed and monitored. Patients must be assured that the use of such technologies does not come at the expense of their privacy.

Developed jointly by the American Health Information Management Association and the Medical Transcription Industry Alliance

Approved by: Board of Directors, American Health Information Management Association

Board of Directors, Medical Transcription Industry Alliance

Date issued: January 1998

Note: Because information security is an issue of importance to both organizations, the American Health Information Management Association (AHIMA) and the Medical Transcription Industry Alliance (MTIA) agreed to collaborate on the development of this joint position statement.

This position statement supports a resolution passed by AHIMA's House of Delegates in October 1996.

EXHIBIT II

The American Health Information Management Association (AHIMA)
Code of Ethical Conduct

The Code of Ethical Conduct is in preliminary form and will be placed before the AHIMA House of Delegates for approval in October 1998.

Preamble: This Code of Ethics sets forth ethical principles for the health information management profession. Members of this profession are responsible for maintaining and promoting ethical practice. This Code of Ethics, when it has been adopted by the American Health Information Management Association, shall be binding on health information management professionals who are members of the Association.

I. Health information management professionals respect the rights and dignity of all individuals.

II. Health information management professionals comply with all laws, regulations, and standards governing the practice of health information management.

III. Health information management professionals discharge responsibility to the best of their ability and strive for professional excellence through self-assessment and continuing education.

IV. Health information management professionals truthfully and accurately represent their professional credentials, education, and experience.

V. Health information management professionals accept the responsibility to protect the public and the profession from unethical, incompetent, or illegal acts.

VI. Health information management professionals promote and protect the confidentiality and security of health records and health information as mandated by law, professional standards, and employers' policies.

VII. Health information management professionals strive to provide accurate and timely information to benefit patients.

VIII. Health information management professionals promote high standards for health information management practice, education, and research.

VIX. Health information management professionals act with integrity and avoid conflict of interest in discharging professional and AHIMA responsibilities.

X. Health information management professionals communicate violations of this Code of Ethics to AHIMA's Professional Conduct Committee.

EXHIBIT III

The American Health Information Management Association (AHIMA)
Standards of Ethical Coding

The standards below were developed by the AHIMA Council on Coding and Classification to give medical coders ethical guidelines for performing their tasks. They are intended to impart the responsibility and importance coders have as members of the healthcare team and to support them as dignified professionals.

In this era of payment based on diagnostic and procedural coding, the professional ethics of medical record coders continue to be challenged. The following standards for ethical coding developed by the AHIMA Council on Coding and Classification and approved by the AHIMA Board of Directors are offered to guide the coder in this process. (The Official ICD-9-CM Coding Guidelines, published by the Cooperating Parties [American Hospital Association, American Health Information Management Association, Health Care Financing Administration, and the National Center for Health Statistics], should be followed in all facilities regardless of payment source.)

1. Diagnoses that are present on admission or diagnoses and procedures that occur during the current encounter are to be abstracted after a thorough review of the entire medical record. Those diagnoses not applicable to the current encounter should not be abstracted.

2. Selection of the principal diagnosis and principal procedure, along with other diagnoses and procedures, must meet the definitions of the Uniform Hospital Discharge Data Set (UHDDS).

3. Assessment must be made of the documentation in the chart to ensure that it is adequate and appropriate to support the diagnoses and procedures selected to be abstracted.

4. Medical record coders should use their skills, their knowledge of ICD-9-CM and CPT, and any available resources to select diagnostic and procedural codes.

5. Medical record coders should not change codes or narratives of codes so that the meanings are misrepresented. Nor should diagnoses or procedures be included or excluded because the payment will be affected. Statistical clinical data is an important result of coding, and maintaining a quality database should be a conscientious goal.

6. Physicians should be consulted for clarification when they enter conflicting or ambiguous documentation in the chart.

7. The medical record coder is a member of the healthcare team, and, as such, should assist physicians who are unfamiliar with ICD-9-CM, CPT or DRG methodology by suggesting resequencing or inclusion of diagnoses or procedures when needed to more accurately reflect the occurrence of events during the encounter.

8. The medical record coder is expected to strive for the optimal payment to which the facility is legally entitled, but it is unethical and illegal to maximize payment by means that contradict regulatory guidelines.

EXHIBIT IV — BUSINESS CARDS

Jane J. Jones, A.R.T.

Coding Specialist
and
Independent Coding Consultant

1000 Oak Tree Avenue   555-555-5555
Sacramento, CA 00000

Mary M. Martin, A.R.T.

Coding Specialist
and
**Independent Coding
Consultant**

2000 Heritage Circle
Indianapolis, IN 00000

555-555-5555

Φ

Specializing in DRG Optimization   *Revenue Recovery*

Susan S. Smith, C.C.S.
Certified Coding Specialist

1500 Success Street   555-555-5555
New York, NY 00000

EXHIBIT V — RECORD COMPLETION LOG

<table>
<tr><td colspan="10" align="center">Susan S. Smith, ART, Coding Consultant
Record Completion Log</td></tr>
<tr><td colspan="6">Hospital_____</td><td colspan="4">Date _____ / ___ / _____</td></tr>
<tr><td rowspan="3">#</td><td rowspan="3">MEDICAL
RECORD
NUMBER</td><td colspan="4" align="center">INPATIENT</td><td colspan="4" align="center">OUTPATIENT</td></tr>
<tr><td>MCare</td><td>Non-
MCare</td><td>>30
Days</td><td>Incom-
plete</td><td>Abstr</td><td>Med</td><td>Surg</td><td>CPT</td></tr>
<tr><td></td><td></td><td></td><td></td><td></td><td></td><td></td><td></td></tr>
<tr><td>1</td><td>- -</td><td></td><td></td><td></td><td></td><td></td><td></td><td></td><td></td></tr>
<tr><td>2</td><td>- -</td><td></td><td></td><td></td><td></td><td></td><td></td><td></td><td></td></tr>
<tr><td>3</td><td>- -</td><td></td><td></td><td></td><td></td><td></td><td></td><td></td><td></td></tr>
<tr><td>4</td><td>- -</td><td></td><td></td><td></td><td></td><td></td><td></td><td></td><td></td></tr>
<tr><td>5</td><td>- -</td><td></td><td></td><td></td><td></td><td></td><td></td><td></td><td></td></tr>
<tr><td>6</td><td>- -</td><td></td><td></td><td></td><td></td><td></td><td></td><td></td><td></td></tr>
<tr><td>7</td><td>- -</td><td></td><td></td><td></td><td></td><td></td><td></td><td></td><td></td></tr>
<tr><td>8</td><td>- -</td><td></td><td></td><td></td><td></td><td></td><td></td><td></td><td></td></tr>
<tr><td>9</td><td>- -</td><td></td><td></td><td></td><td></td><td></td><td></td><td></td><td></td></tr>
<tr><td>10</td><td>- -</td><td></td><td></td><td></td><td></td><td></td><td></td><td></td><td></td></tr>
<tr><td>11</td><td>- -</td><td></td><td></td><td></td><td></td><td></td><td></td><td></td><td></td></tr>
<tr><td>12</td><td>- -</td><td></td><td></td><td></td><td></td><td></td><td></td><td></td><td></td></tr>
<tr><td>13</td><td>- -</td><td></td><td></td><td></td><td></td><td></td><td></td><td></td><td></td></tr>
<tr><td>14</td><td>- -</td><td></td><td></td><td></td><td></td><td></td><td></td><td></td><td></td></tr>
<tr><td>15</td><td>- -</td><td></td><td></td><td></td><td></td><td></td><td></td><td></td><td></td></tr>
<tr><td>16</td><td>- -</td><td></td><td></td><td></td><td></td><td></td><td></td><td></td><td></td></tr>
<tr><td>17</td><td>- -</td><td></td><td></td><td></td><td></td><td></td><td></td><td></td><td></td></tr>
<tr><td>18</td><td>- -</td><td></td><td></td><td></td><td></td><td></td><td></td><td></td><td></td></tr>
<tr><td>19</td><td>- -</td><td></td><td></td><td></td><td></td><td></td><td></td><td></td><td></td></tr>
<tr><td>20</td><td>- -</td><td></td><td></td><td></td><td></td><td></td><td></td><td></td><td></td></tr>
<tr><td>21</td><td>- -</td><td></td><td></td><td></td><td></td><td></td><td></td><td></td><td></td></tr>
<tr><td>22</td><td>- -</td><td></td><td></td><td></td><td></td><td></td><td></td><td></td><td></td></tr>
<tr><td>23</td><td>- -</td><td></td><td></td><td></td><td></td><td></td><td></td><td></td><td></td></tr>
<tr><td>24</td><td>- -</td><td></td><td></td><td></td><td></td><td></td><td></td><td></td><td></td></tr>
<tr><td>25</td><td>- -</td><td></td><td></td><td></td><td></td><td></td><td></td><td></td><td></td></tr>
<tr><td></td><td>TOTAL</td><td></td><td></td><td></td><td></td><td></td><td></td><td></td><td></td></tr>
</table>

EXHIBIT VI — DRG CONTRACTING WORKSHEET FOR CHART REVIEW

CAPITOL CODING CENTER
JANE J. JONES, CCS

ACCOUNT # _____

MR # _____

D/S DATE _____

ORIGINAL CODING	RE-CODING
P. DX	P.DX

_____ _____   _____ _____

_____ _____   _____ _____

_____ _____   _____ _____

_____ _____   _____ _____

_____ _____   _____ _____

_____ _____   _____ _____

PROCEDURE CODES	PROCEDURE CODES

_____ _____   _____ _____

_____ _____   _____ _____

_____ _____   _____ _____

_____ _____   _____ _____

DRG _____   DRG _____

WT. _____   WT. _____

PAYMENT $_____   PAYMENT $_____

INCREASE PAYMENT $_____

Reason(s) for Recommended Change(s) and/or Comments:

_____

_____

_____

_____

EXHIBIT VII — DRG OPTIMIZATION WORKSHEET

OPTIMIZATION WORKSHEET

_____
Hospital

NAME: _____   REVIEW DATE: _____

MED RECORD #: _____   PHYSICIAN: _____

DISC DATE: _____   DISC STATUS: _____

	Hospital Code	New Code	Description
Principal Diagnosis 1-	_____	_____	_____
Secondary Diagnosis 2-	_____	_____	_____
3-	_____	_____	_____
4-	_____	_____	_____
5-	_____	_____	_____
Principal Procedure 1-	_____	_____	_____
Secondary Procedures 2-	_____	_____	_____
3-	_____	_____	_____

DRG _____   Increase Relative Weight _____

Relative Weight _____

Blended _____   Reimbursement Increase _____

Payment _____

> **"AFTER STUDY" THE PRINCIPAL DIAGNOSIS**
> 1) Present on Admission
> 2) Acute or Subacute
> 3) Treated or Addressed
> 4) Most Severe
> 5) Most Resource Intensive
> 6) Highest R.W.

Comments E.R. _____

Hx _____

P.E. _____

Lab _____

X-Ray _____

EKG _____

Misc. _____

INCREASE LEVEL OF SERVICE for CPT BILLING:

INCREASE COMPLEXITY from	LOW	MODERATE	HIGH
	<.6000;	.6000 - .7999;	.8000>

JUSTIFIED INCREASE LOS from____ days to ____ GAINED____

254

EXHIBIT VIII — DRG OPTIMIZATION SUMMARY WORKSHEET

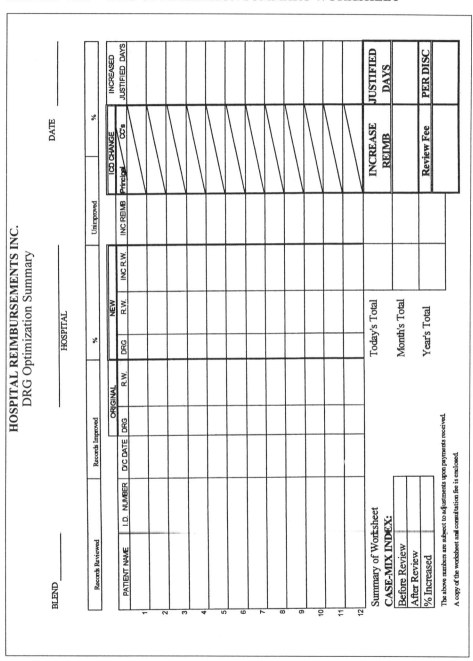

HOSPITAL REIMBURSEMENTS INC.
DRG Optimization Summary

BLEND _____   Records Reviewed _____   Records Improved _____   %_____   Unimproved _____   %_____   DATE _____

HOSPITAL _____

PATIENT NAME	I.D. NUMBER	D/C DATE	ORIGINAL DRG	R.W.	%	NEW DRG	R.W.	INC R.W.	INC REIMB	ICD CHANGE Principal	CCs	INCREASED JUSTIFIED DAYS
1												
2												
3												
4												
5												
6												
7												
8												
9												
10												
11												
12												

Summary of Worksheet   Today's Total   INCREASE REIMB   JUSTIFIED DAYS
CASE-MIX INDEX:
Before Review   Month's Total
After Review   Year's Total   Review Fee   PER DISC
% Increased

The above numbers are subject to adjustments upon payments received

A copy of the worksheet and consultation fee is enclosed

255

EXHIBIT IX — INVOICE FORM FOR DRG CONTRACTING

CAPITOL CODING CENTER

Jane J. Jones, CCS
1000 Oak Tree Avenue
Sacramento, CA 00000
555-555-5555

INVOICE #
DATE:
Blended Rate $

ACCT #	MR #	D/S DATE	ORIG. DRG/WT	REVISED DRG/WT	WT INCREASE	$ PMT INCREASE	% DIFFERENTIAL
					Total wt. inc.	Total Payment $ inc.	Total % Differential
					Wt.	$	$

PAYMENT DUE $ _____

256

EXHIBIT X — PERSONAL TIME SHEET

CAPITOL CODING CENTER
PERSONAL TIME SHEET

NAME _____ PAY PERIOD _____

DATE	TIME IN	TIME OUT	TIME IN	TIME OUT	WORKED HOURS	TOTAL HOURS
Sun.						
Mon.						
Tues.						
Wed.						
Thurs.						
Fri.						
Sat.						
Sun.						
Mon.						
Tues.						
Weds.						
Thurs.						
Fri.						
Sat.						
Totals						

EXHIBIT XI— BILLING/INVOICE FORM I

Susan S. Smith, ART
Coding Service
P.O. Box 1000
Fairview, Fl 00000
(555-555-5555)

Date ___ / ___ / ___

To _____

Address _____

City _____

EXHIBIT XII — BILLING/INVOICE FORM II

CAPITOL CODING CENTER
Jane J. Jones, CCS
1000 Oak Tree Avenue
Sacramento, CA 00000
555-555-5555

INVOICE #   DATE:

FOR SERVICES RENDERED TO: Happy Hollow Hospital
                                        Site Name

Name _____
Social Security # _____
Actual days on site _____
                              dates
Total hours worked   _____   @$XX.XX per hour =
Mileage per pay period   _____   @$.XX/mile   =
Meals per pay period   _____   @$XX./day   =

     HOURS WORKED PER DAY   _____

Days on site   Date   Hours per day

Monday   _____   _____
Tuesday   _____   _____
Wednesday   _____   _____
Thursday   _____   _____
Friday   _____   _____
Saturday   _____   _____
Sunday   _____   _____

          TOTAL DUE THIS INVOICE _____

Signature of contractor _____
Address of contractor   _____
_____
Authorized signature for payment

   GL Acct.#   _____
   CK# _____ Date Paid_____

259

EXHIBIT XIII

SERVICES AGREEMENT FOR CONTRACT CODING

TERMS OF AGREEMENT

This agreement, dated _____, 199 __ , is entered into between __**Your company name**__ and ___**Hospital name**_____ , _____**City**_____ , _____**State**_____ , hereinafter called "Hospital". This agreement shall be binding on both ____**Your company name**____ and the Hospital and shall continue indefinitely or until mutually amended. This contract can be terminated by either party by providing a thirty day written notice.

SCOPE OF WORK

Your company name agrees to provide contract coding services to the Medical Record Department of the Hospital. The services shall include performing ICD-9 and CPT coding and abstracting of inpatient, ambulatory surgery, emergency room, and referred outpatient medical records.

Your company name shall perform its services according to current regulations and guidelines set forth for ICD-9 and CPT coding by WHO and AMA and approved by HCFA and JCAHO. **Your company name** shall be responsible for correcting any errors or omissions brought to its attention during the term of this agreement.

INDEMNIFICATION

Each party agrees to indemnify and hold harmless the other with respect to all claims, costs (including reasonable attorney's fees), damages, fines, or losses caused or alleged to have been caused by the acts, omissions, or negligence of the indemnifying party, its agents, employees or representatives.

WORK SCHEDULE

The frequency of on-site coding and the specific work schedule shall be agreed upon between the Hospital Medical Records Director and **Your company name**.

CONFIDENTIALITY

Your company name will not release any confidential patient, physician, or hospital information to any individual.

HOSPITAL / YOUR COMPANY NAME RELATIONSHIP

The Hospital and **Your company name** agree that their relationship is that of an individual contractor and not as employer and employee. **Your company name** acknowledges that it has no right, entitlement or claim against the Hospital for employer taxes, social security benefits, worker's compensation benefits, retirement, vacation leaves, sick leave or any other employee benefit of any kind.

Hospital shall compensate **Your company name** as follows:

Contract coding fee: $____ per hour (or per chart)
Travel expenses as follows:

     Motel room: Actual cost
     Mileage allowance: $.26 per mile to and from the facility
     Meal allowance: $20.00 per day

PAYMENT

Payment shall be made to **Your company name** within two weeks of presentation of a bill for services.

FORMALIZATION

The covenants, representation and services set forth herein on behalf of the parties are agreed to on the date specified above under "Terms of Agreement". This agreement shall be construed and interpreted under the laws of the **your state**. This written agreement and any subsequent amendments mutually agreed to in writing and signed by the Hospital and **Your company name** reflect the entire agreement between the Hospital and **Your company name**.

Your company name   **Hospital name**

_____   _____
Signature   *Signature*
Your name and title   **Hospital representative's name and title**

_____   _____
Date   **Date**

EXHIBIT XIV

MEDICAL RECORDS CODING CONTRACT

This agreement entered into this____day of _____ , 199_, by and between the subcontractor known as ____**Your company name**____ , herein referred to as SUBCONTRACTOR, whose address is _____**Full address**_____ , and the contractor known as ____**Medical facility's name**____ , herein referred to as CONTRACTOR:

WHEREAS SUBCONTRACTOR desires to contract with CONTRACTOR to perform medical records coding services, and whereas the parties desire to set forth their contractual and business arrangements; therefore, this agreement constitutes the said contractual and business arrangements, and the parties contract and agree as follows:

Independent contractor

Subcontractor shall be an independent contractor at all times in the performance of this agreement. It is agreed that neither party is an agent or an employee of the other. Subcontractor has control of the sequence of tasks that lead to the completion of the required services. Subcontractor decides when and where the required services shall be performed, abiding by guidelines for completion dates and report format set by contractor.

Pricing and payment

1. Client pricing is set and agreed to as in attachment, schedule A, FEE SCHEDULE. Payment for services rendered is on a monthly basis. The SUBCONTRACTOR is responsible to issue a billing to the CONTRACTOR on the first (1st) of each month for the first (1st) through the thirty-first (31st)

day of the prior month. Payment to the SUBCONTRACTOR from the CONTRACTOR is due on or before the tenth (10th) of the month for the period of the first (1st) through the thirty-first (31st).

2. Charts will be furnished in original condition with all available information attached. An additional fee (see attachment, Schedule A, FEE SCHEDULE) will be applied if SUBCONTRACTOR organizes or locates information and compiles charts.

Termination

Violation of any part of this contract can result in termination by either party without notice if said violations are not corrected within five (5) working days.

The subcontractor, __**Your company name**_____ , and the contractor, ___**Medical facility's name**_____ , hereby agree to abide by all terms and stipulations set forth and understand each item fully, as signified by signing below.

Signature
_____
**Your company name and
Your name and title**

Signature
_____
**Medical facility's name and
Representative's name and title**

_____
DATE

EXHIBIT XV

SCHEDULE A
FEE SCHEDULE

CODING ICD-9-CM
CPT as needed

INPATIENT DISCHARGES

Medicare — coding and abstracting	$X.XX/ chart
Non-Medicare — coding and abstracting	$X.XX/ chart

OUTPATIENT SURGERY

Discharges — ICD-9-CM plus CPT/ abstracting	$X.XX/ chart

UNASSEMBLED/LOOSE FILING ORGANIZATION

Inpatient charts — organizing and collating	$ X.XX/ chart

EXHIBIT XVI

SCHEDULE B
NONDISCLOSURE AGREEMENT

By signing this Non-Disclosure Agreement, I indicate my understanding that:

Patients, physicians and other health care providers furnish confidential information to obtain or carry out medical services and that medical service information and records are confidential.

Patients depend on the providers of medical services to keep patient information confidential. The provider's reputation depends on this confidentiality.

If medical information has been used or disclosed inappropriately, patients or providers who have suffered loss or injury may seek legal remedy to recover damages from the person who used or disclosed this information. Specific violations of patient confidentiality resulting in economic loss or personal injury to a patient my be punishable by law.

Any breach of confidentiality will be considered serious and subject to investigation and possible disciplinary action, including immediate termination of services.

Therefore, as a contract service provider, I agree that I will not at any time:

1. Disclose services given or information about patients.

2. Allow anyone else to examine or copy any records or documents having to do with patients, physicians, or other health care providers and services.

_____
**Your company name and
your name and title**

DATE _____

Index

G

outpatient 3, 15, 23, 24, 28, 32, 35, 53-54, 67, 68, 76, 82-85, 102, 103-104, 106, 109, 123, 125, 148, 156-157, 159, 211
open-end lease 180
optimize/optimizers/optimizing 1, 8, 17, 61, 62, 66, 126, 129, 144, 145, 239
Opus 23, 44, 118, 219

P

pathology reports 148-149
paying yourself 183-184
PcAnywhere 84
per-chart fees 101, 102, 103, 125
physician office 2, 11, 28, 33, 80, 81, 82, 84, 87, 126, 221
Picture Archiving and Communication System 209
planning 7, 8, 11, 33, 49, 67, 93, 95, 98, 135, 196, 205, 239
policies and procedures, definition 239
priorities 20, 135, 144
procedural terminology 7, 19, 51, 52, 231
ProComm Plus 84
productivity 20-21, 70, 93, 95, 102, 103, 124, 129, 136, 153
Professional Edition 216
professional liability 157
professional organizations 12, 22-23, 24, 25, 35, 36, 137
Prospective Payment System (PPS) 6, 7, 53, 54, 55, 56, 57, 62, 129, 134, 145
provider, definition 241
Public Health Service 4, 5, 6
psychiatric hospitals 110

Q

quality coding 8, 17, 18, 27, 31, 33-34, 60, 70, 73, 75, 80, 125, 126, 144, 146, 148, 149, 151
quality assurance (QA) 8, 80, 227, 238
qualified profit sharing plans 202

R

Rayve Productions 204
record retention 158
recovery specialist 39, 90, 91
reference books and materials 38, 40, 84, 89, 172

T

target market 11, 105, 106, 107
taxes
    deposits 189-191
    federal 186-188
    home 194-197
    preparer 204, 205
    returns 158, 193, 205
    sheltering 202
    Social Security 191-192
    state 193
    types of 185-186
technical skills 1, 10, 11, 15, 16, 18, 21, 28, 31, 38, 55, 111, 126, 130, 133, 136
technology updates 207-210
telephone 95, 152, 157, 178, 185, 186, 196, 229
Ten Tips to Inspire Confidence 118
terminology, medical and procedural 7, 16, 19, 38, 39, 40, 48, 51, 52, 72, 83, 84, 231
The Coding Edge 217
The Coding Registry 218
The Educational Annotation 217
The Expanded ICD-9-CM 217
The One Minute Manager 152
The Small Business Directory 172
The Surgical Cross-Coder 219
Time to Code 215
travel expenses 170, 200
tumor registry 87, 88, 89, 90

U

unbilled list/accounts 125, 126
unethical coding 140, 141, 143
United States General Services Administration 188
United States Government Printing Office 186
upcoding 145

V

verbal contracts 123

W

X-Y-Z

ABOUT RAYVE PRODUCTIONS

Rayve Productions is an award-winning small publisher of books and music. Current publications are primarily in the following categories:

(1) Business guidebooks for home-based businesses and other entrepreneurs
(2) Quality children's books and music
(3) History books about America and her regions, and an heirloom-quality journal for creating personal histories.

Rayve Productions' mail-order catalog offers the above items plus business books, software, music, and other enjoyable items produced by others.

Our eclectic collection of business resources and gift items has something to please everyone.

A FREE catalog is available upon request.

Come visit us at www.spannet.org/rayve.

BUSINESS & CAREER

☆ *Smart Tax Write-offs, 2nd edition: Hundreds of tax deduction ideas for home-based businesses, independent contractors, all entrepreneurs*   by Norm Ray, CPA
ISBN 1-877810-19-3, softcover, $12.95, 1999 pub.
Fun-to-read, easy-to-use guidebook that encourages entrepreneurs to be aggressive and creative in taking legitimate tax deductions. Includes valuable checklist of over 600 write-off ideas. Every small business owner's "must read."
(Recommended by *Home Office Computing, Small Business Opportunities, Spare Time, Independent Business Magazine.*)

☆ *The Independent Medical Transcriptionist, 3rd edition: The comprehensive guidebook for career success in a home-based medical transcription business*
by Donna Avila-Weil, CMT, and Mary Glaccum, CMT
ISBN 1-877810-23-1, softcover, $34.95, 1998 pub.
The industry's premier reference book for medical transcription entrepreneurs.
(Recommended by *Journal of the American Association for Medical Transcription, Entrepreneur, Small Business Opportunities*)

☆ *Independent Medical Coding: The comprehensive guidebook for career success as a home-based medical coder*
by Donna Avila-Weil, CMT and Rhonda Regan, CCS
ISBN 1-877810-17-7, softcover, $34.95, 1999 pub.
How to start and successfully run your own professional independent medical coding business. Step-by-step instructions.

☆ *Nationwide Medical Transcription Service Directory: The most comprehensive published listing of medical transcription service professionals in the United States*
compiled by Denise M. Schultheis
ISBN 1-877810-67-3, softcover, $24.95, 1998 pub.
This premier directory contains more than 600 medical transcription service professionals throughout the United States with many listings expanded to include types of services offered, specialties and other useful information.

☆ *Easy Financials for Your Home-based Business*   by Norm Ray, CPA
ISBN 1-877810-92-4, softcover, $19.95, 1992 pub.
Small business & home-based business expert helps you save time by making your work easier, and save money by nailing down your tax deductions.
(Recommended by *Wilson Library Bulletin, The Business Journal, National Home Business Report*)

☆ *Internal Medicine Words*   by Minta Danna

ISBN 1-877810-68-1, softcover, $29.95, 1997 pub.

More than 8,000 words and terms related to internal medicine. A valuable spelling and terminology usage resource for medical transcriptionists, medical writers and editors, court reporters, medical records personnel, and others working with medical documentation.

☆ *Shrinking the Globe into Your Company's Hands: The step-by-step international trade guide for small businesses*   by Sidney R. Lawrence, PE

ISBN 1-877810-46-0, softcover, $24.95, 1997 pub.

An expert in foreign trade shows U.S. small business owners how to market and export products and services safely and profitably.

HISTORY

☆ *20 Tales of California: A rare collection of western stories*   by Hector Lee

ISBN 1-877810-62-2, softcover, $9.95, 1998 pub.

Mysterious and romantic tales: real life and folklore set in various California locations. Includes ideas for family outings and classroom field trips.

☆ *Link Across America: A story of the historic Lincoln Highway* — see Children's Books

☆ *Windsor, The Birth of a City*   by Gabriel A. Fraire

ISBN 1-877810-91-6, hardcover, $21.95, 1991 pub.

Fascinating case study of political and social issues surrounding city incorporation of Windsor, California, 1978—1991. LAFCO impact.

☆ *LifeTimes, The Life Experiences Journal*

ISBN 1-877810-34-7, hardcover, $49.95

World's easiest, most fun and useful personal journal. Handsome heirloom quality with gilt-edged pages. Over 150 information categories to record your life experiences. Winner of national award for excellence.

COOKBOOK

☆ *Nancy's Candy Cookbook: How to make candy at home the easy way*

by Nancy Shipman

ISBN 1-877810-65-7, softcover, $14.95, 1996 pub.

Have fun and save money by making candy at home at a fraction of candy store prices. More than 100 excellent candy recipes — from Grandma's delicious old-fashioned fudge to modern gourmet truffles. Includes many children's favorites, too.

PARENTING

☆ *Joy of Reading: One family's fun-filled guide to reading success*

by Debbie Duncan

ISBN 1-877810-45-2, softcover, $14.95, 1998 pub.

A dynamic author and mother, and an expert on children's literature, shares her family's personal reading success stories. You'll be inspired and entertained by this lighthearted, candid glimpse into one family's daily experiences as they cope with the ups and downs of life. Through it all, there is love, and an abundance of wonderful books. *More than 600 children's books featured. Learn how to inspire your children to read for pleasure and much more.*

CHILDREN'S BOOKS & MUSIC

☆ *Link Across America: A story of the historic Lincoln Highway*

by Mary Elizabeth Anderson

ISBN 1-877810-97-5, hardcover, $14.95, 1997 pub.

It began with a long-ago dream . . . a road that would run clear across America! The dream became reality in 1914 as the Lincoln Highway began to take form, to eventually run from New York City to San Francisco. Venture from past to present experiencing transportation history. Topics include Abraham Lincoln, teams of horses, seedling miles, small towns, making concrete, auto courts, Burma Shave signs, classic cars and road rallies. Color photos along today's Lincoln Highway remnants, b/w historical photos, map and list of cities along the old Lincoln Highway. (Ages 7-13 & their parents, grandparents and great-grandparents)

☆ *The Perfect Orange: A tale from Ethiopia*

by Frank P. Araujo, PhD; illustrated by Xiao Jun Li

ISBN 1-877810-94-0, hardcover, $16.95, 1994 pub., Toucan Tales volume 2

Inspiring gentle folktale. Breathtaking watercolors dramatize ancient Ethiopia's contrasting pastoral charm and majesty. Illustrations are rich with Ethiopian details. Story reinforces values of generosity and selflessness over greed and self-centeredness. Glossary of Ethiopian terms and pronunciation key.

(PBS *Storytime* Selection; Recommended by *School Library Journal, Faces, MultiCultural Review, Small Press Magazine, The Five Owls, Wilson Library Bulletin)*

☆ *Nekane, the Lamiña & the Bear: A tale of the Basque Pyrenees*

by Frank P. Araujo, PhD; illustrated by Xiao Jun Li

ISBN 1-877810-01-0, hardcover, $16.95, 1993 pub., Toucan Tales volume 1

Delightful Basque folktale pits appealing, quick-witted young heroine against mysterious villain. Lively, imaginative narrative, sprinkled with Basque phrases. Vibrant watercolor images. Glossary of Basque terms and pronunciation key.

(Recommended by School Library Journal, Publishers Weekly, Kirkus Reviews, Booklist, Wilson Library Bulletin, The Basque Studies Program Newsletter: University of Nevada, BCCB, The Five Owls)

☆ The Laughing River: A folktale for peace

by Elizabeth Haze Vega; illustrated by Ashley Smith

ISBN 1-877810-35-5 hardcover book, $16.95, 1995 pub.

ISBN 1-877810-36-3 companion musical audiotape, $9.95

ISBN 1-877810-37-1 book & musical audiotape combo, $23.95

Drum kit, $9.95

Book, musical audiotape & drum kit combo, $29.95

Two fanciful African tribes are in conflict until the laughing river bubbles melodiously into their lives, bringing fun, friendship, peace. Lyrical fanciful folktale of conflict resolution. Mesmerizing music. Dancing, singing and drumming instructions. Orff approach.

(Recommended by *School Library Journal*)

☆ When Molly Was in the Hospital: A book for brothers and sisters of hospitalized children

by Debbie Duncan; illustrated by Nina Ollikainen, MD

ISBN 1-877810-44-4, hardcover, $12.95, 1994 pub.

Anna's little sister, Molly, has been very ill and had to have an operation. Anna tells us all about the experience from her point of view. Sensitive, insightful, heartwarming story. A support and comfort for siblings and those who love them. Authentic. Realistic. Effective.

(**Winner of 1995 Benjamin Franklin Award: Best Children's Picture Book**. Recommended by *Children's Book Insider, School Library Journal, Disabilities Resources Monthly*)

☆ Night Sounds

by Lois G. Grambling; illustrated by Randall F. Ray

ISBN 1-877810-77-0, hardcover, $12.95   ISBN 1-877810-83-5, softcover, $6.95, 1996 pub.

Perfect bedtime story. Ever so gently, a child's thoughts slip farther and farther away, moving from purring cat at bedside and comical creatures in the yard to distant trains and church bells, and then at last, to sleep. Imaginative, lilting text and daringly unpretentious b/w watercolor illustrations

☆ Los Sonidos de la Noche

by Lois G. Grambling; illustrated by Randall F. Ray

(Spanish edition of *Night Sounds*), 1996 pub.

ISBN 1-877810-76-2, hardcover, $12.95   ISBN 1-877810-82-7, softcover, $6.95

ORDER

For mail orders, please complete this order form and forward with check, money order or credit card information to Rayve Productions, POB 726, Windsor CA 95492. If paying with a credit card, you can call us toll-free at 800.852.4890 or fax this completed form to Rayve Productions at 707.838.2220.

You can also order at our web site at www.spannet.org/rayve.

☐ Please send me the following book(s):

Title	Price	Qty	Amount
Title	Price	Qty	Amount
Title	Price	Qty	Amount
Title	Price	Qty	Amount
Title	Price	Qty	Amount

Total Amount _____

Sales Tax: Californians please add 7.5% sales tax

Sales Tax _____

S/H: Book rate — $3.50 for first book + $.75 each additional
Priority — $4.50 for first book + $1 each additional
UPS — $1.50 plus actual UPS charge

Shipping _____

Total _____

Name _____ Phone _____

Address _____

City State Zip _____

☐ Check enclosed $ _____   Date _____

☐ Charge my Visa/MC/Discover/AMEX $ _____

Credit card # _____   Exp. _____

Signature _____   *Thank you!*

Cod

ORDER

For mail orders, please complete this order form and forward with check, money order or credit card information to Rayve Productions, POB 726, Windsor CA 95492. If paying with a credit card, you can call us toll-free at 800.852.4890 or fax this completed form to Rayve Productions at 707.838.2220.

You can also order at our web site at www.spannet.org/rayve.

☐ Please send me the following book(s):

Title	Price	Qty	Amount
Title	Price	Qty	Amount
Title	Price	Qty	Amount
Title	Price	Qty	Amount
Title	Price	Qty	Amount

Total Amount _____

Sales Tax: Californians please add 7.5% sales tax

Sales Tax _____

S/H: Book rate — $3.50 for first book + $.75 each additional
Priority — $4.50 for first book + $1 each additional
UPS — $1.50 plus actual UPS charge

Shipping _____

Total _____

Name _____ Phone _____

Address _____

City State Zip _____

☐ Check enclosed $ _____   Date _____

☐ Charge my Visa/MC/Discover/AMEX $ _____

Credit card # _____   Exp. _____

Signature _____ *Thank you!*

Cod